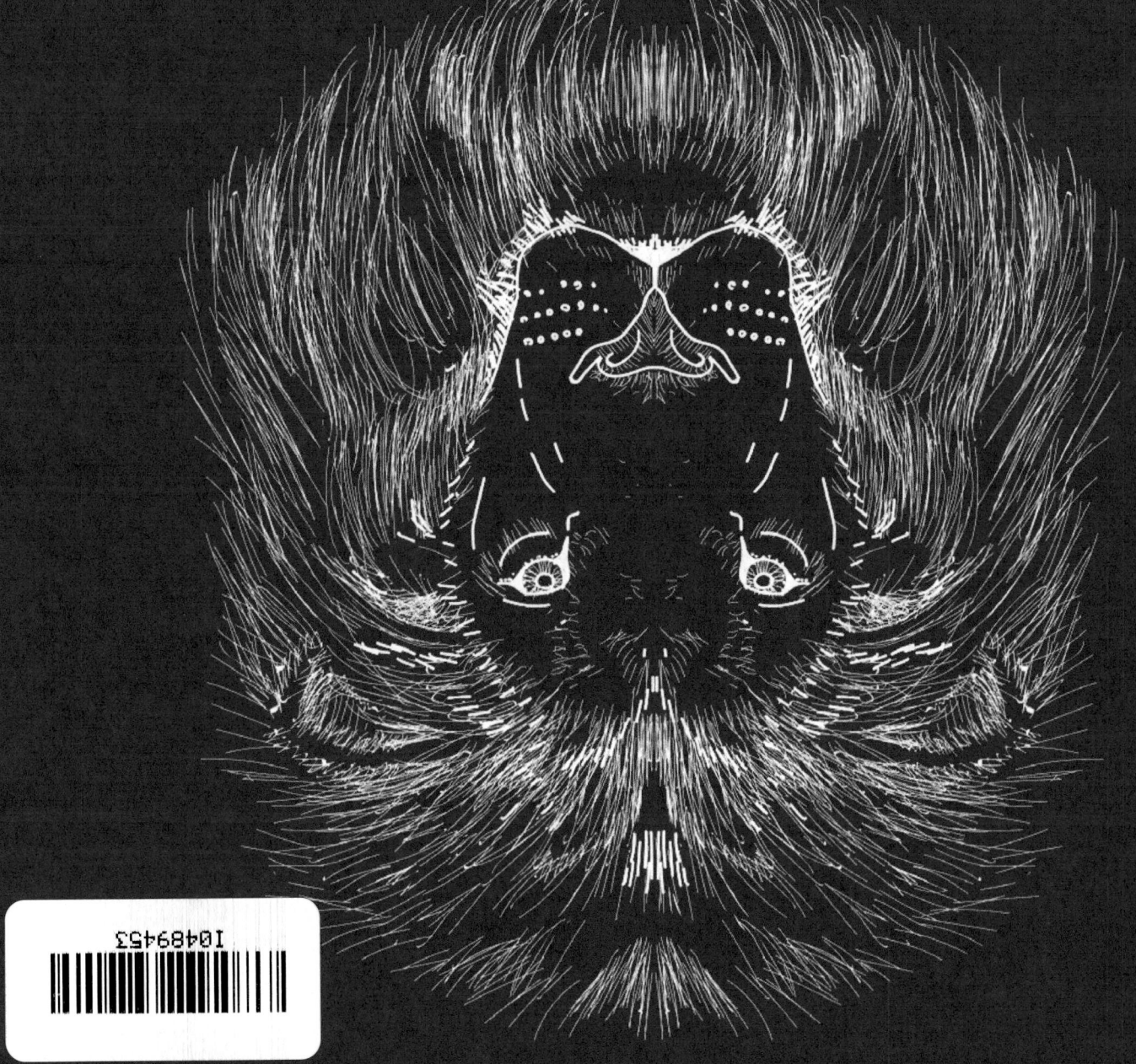

ADULT COLORING BOOK

Stress relief for all ages.

REAL PHOTOS OF THE AFRICAN CONTINENT.

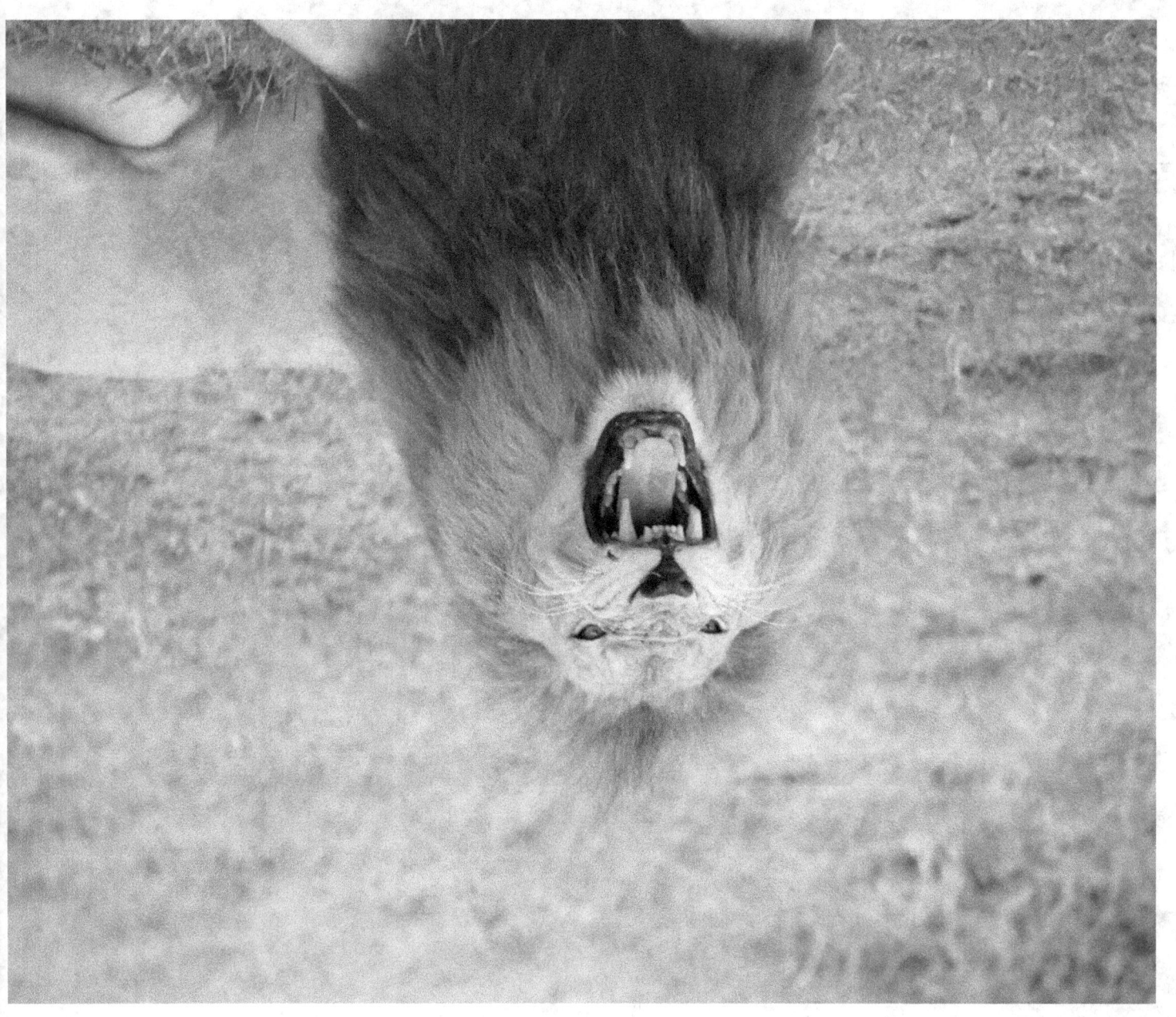

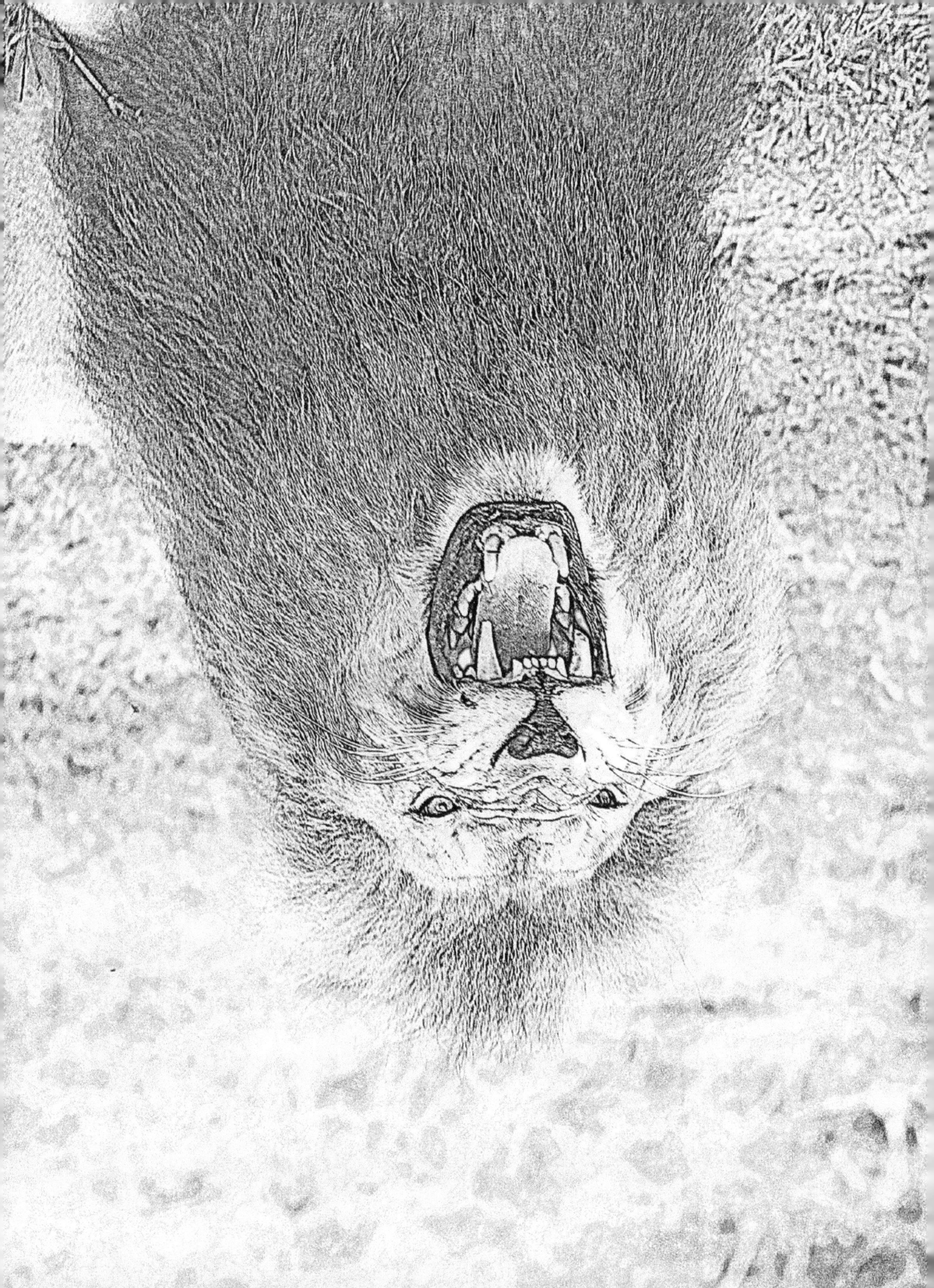

"OPTIMISM IS THE ONE QUALITY MORE ASSOCIATED WITH SUCCESS AND HAPPINESS THAN ANY OTHER."

- BRIAN TRACY

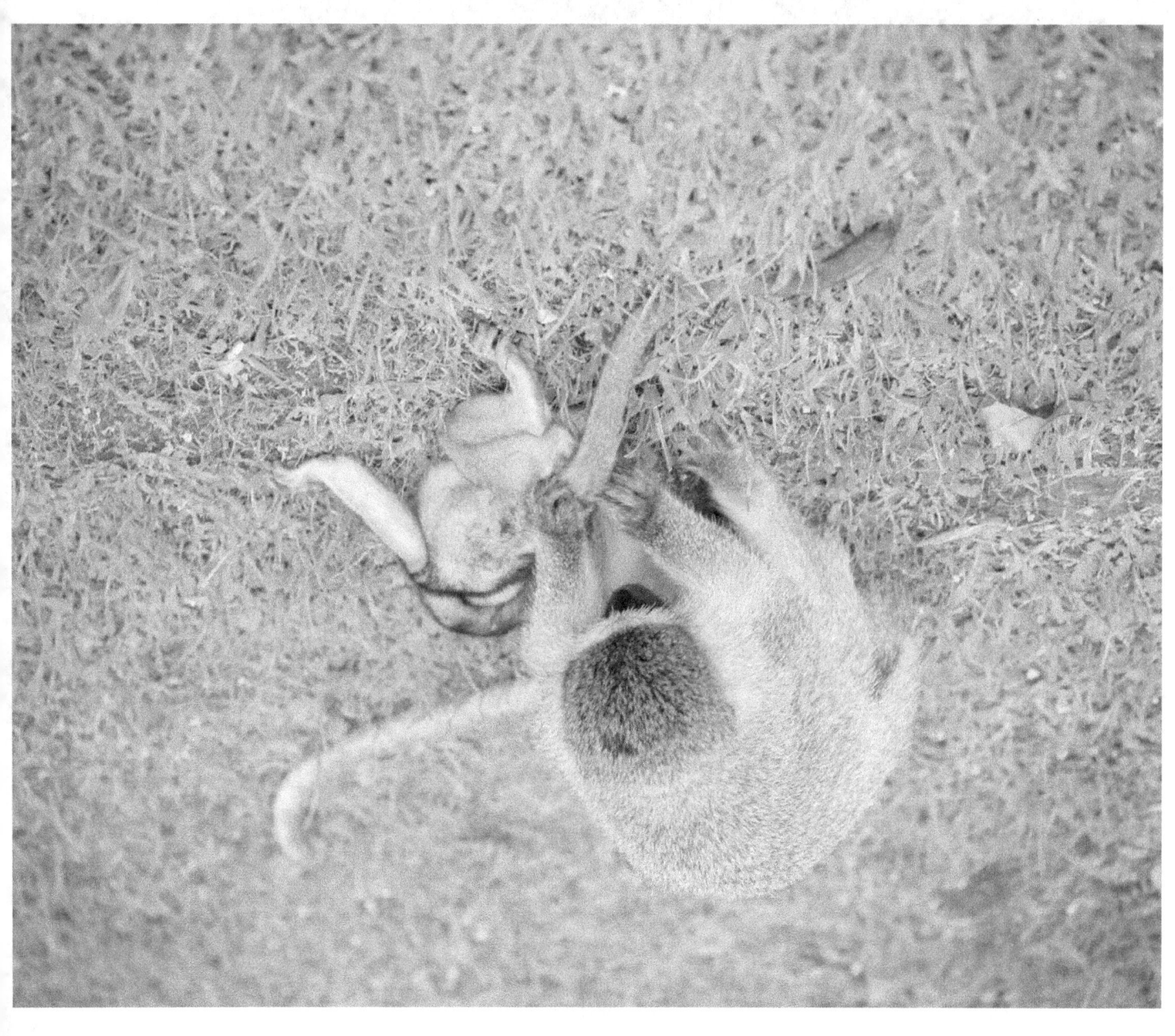

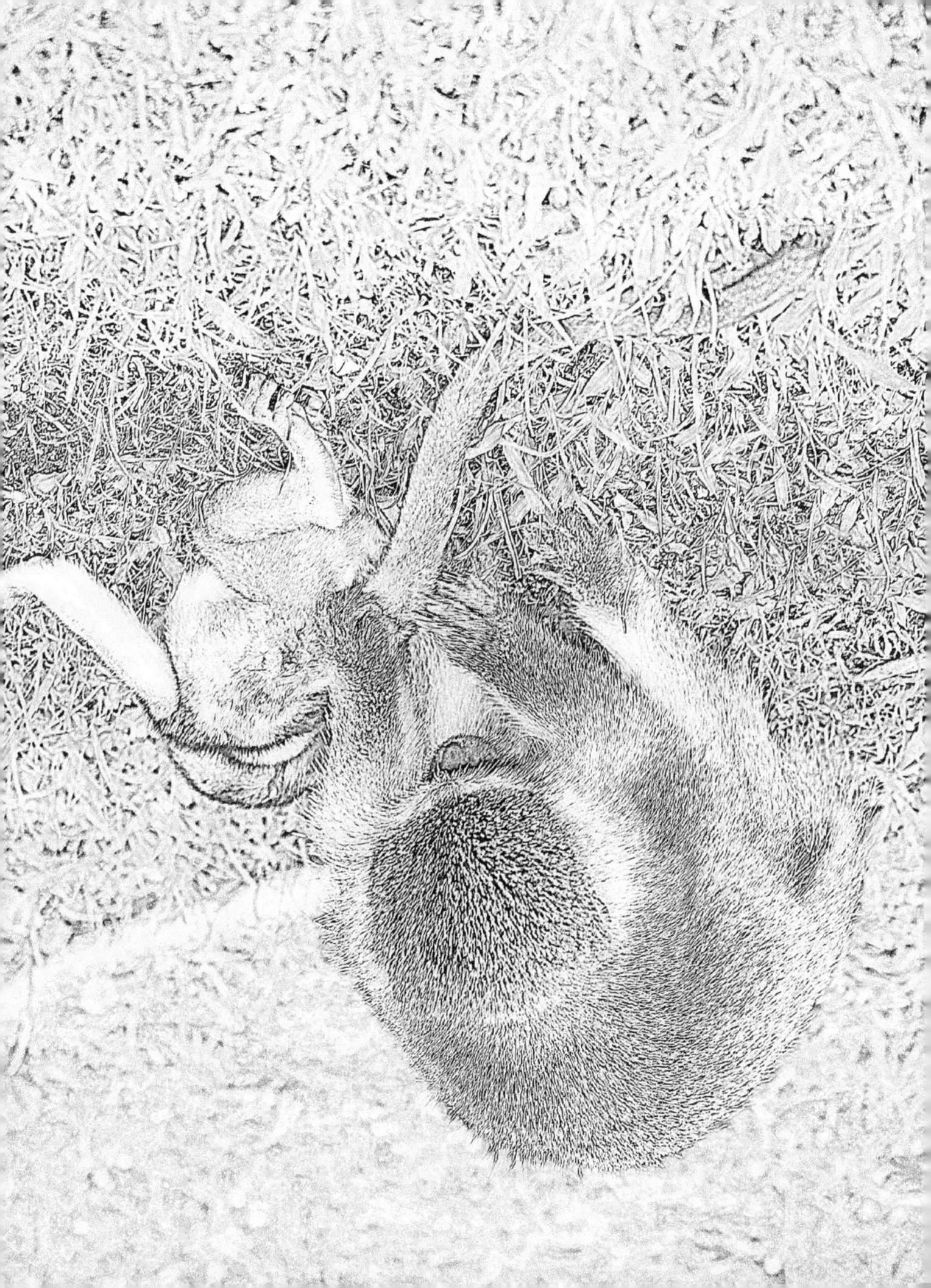

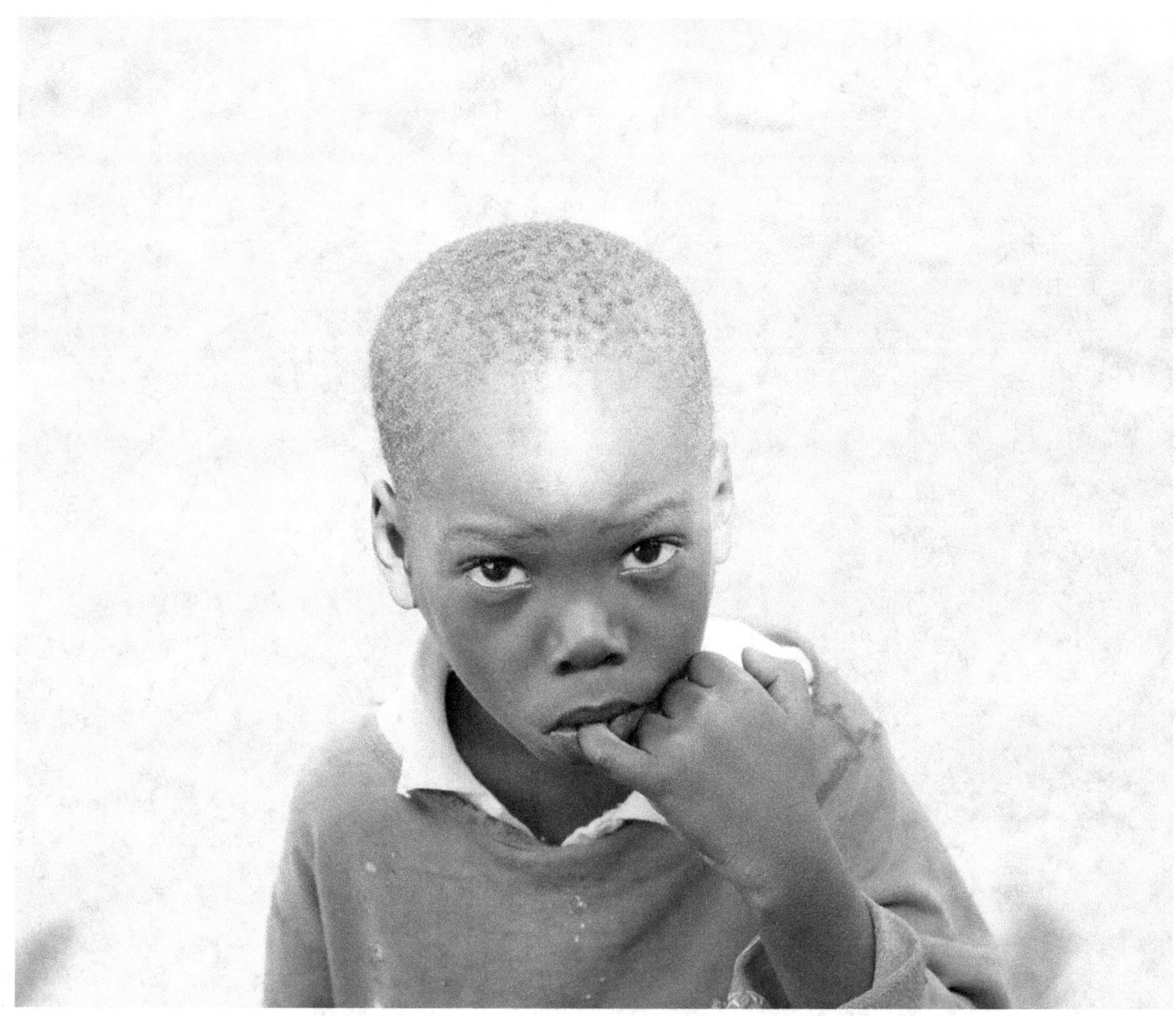

"ALWAYS KEEP YOUR EYES OPEN. KEEP WATCHING. BECAUSE WHATEVER YOU SEE CAN INSPIRE YOU."
- GRACE CODDINGTON

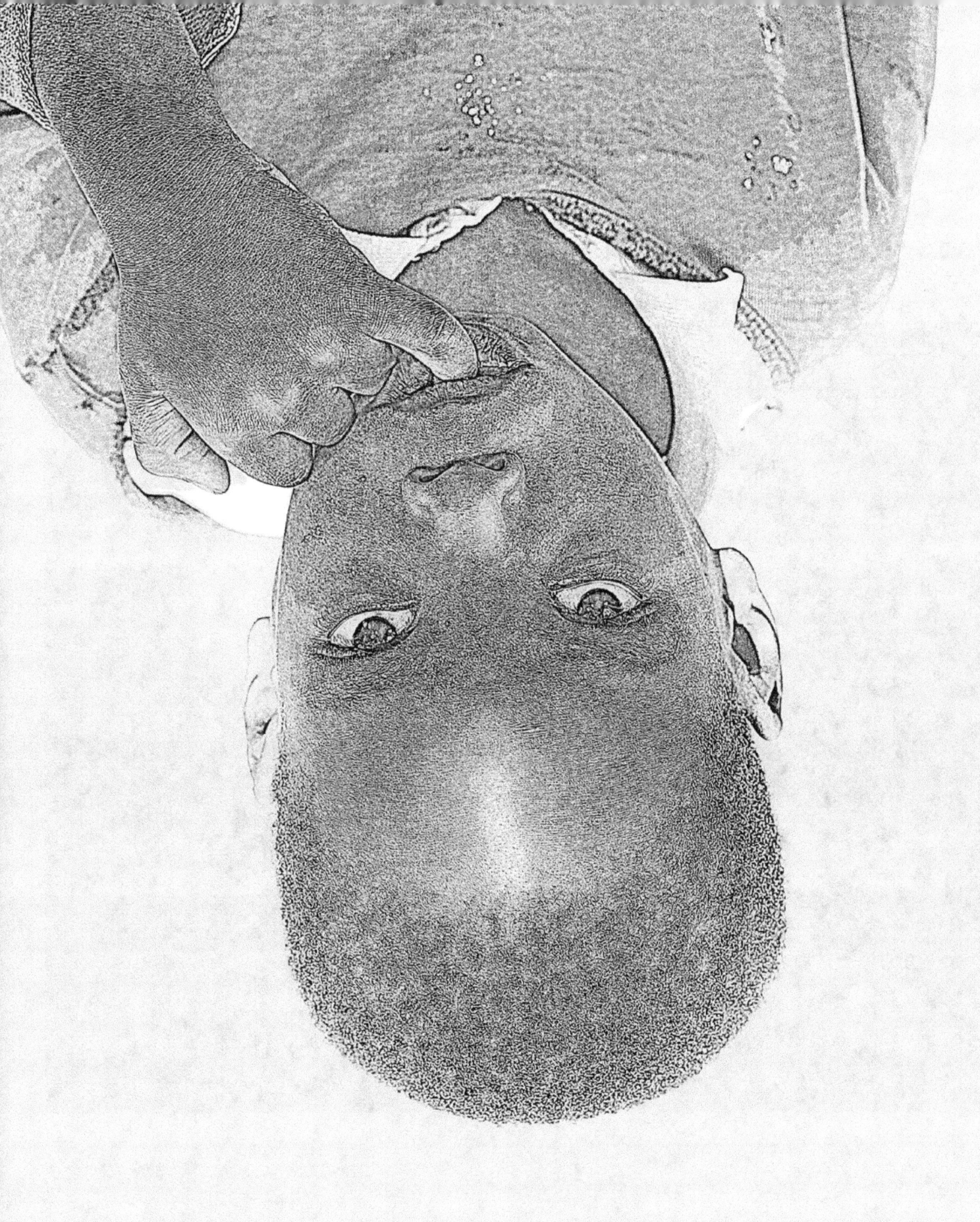

"WHAT YOU GET BY ACHIEVING YOUR GOALS IS NOT AS IMPORTANT AS WHAT YOU
BECOME BY ACHIEVING YOUR GOALS."
- HENRY DAVID THOREAU

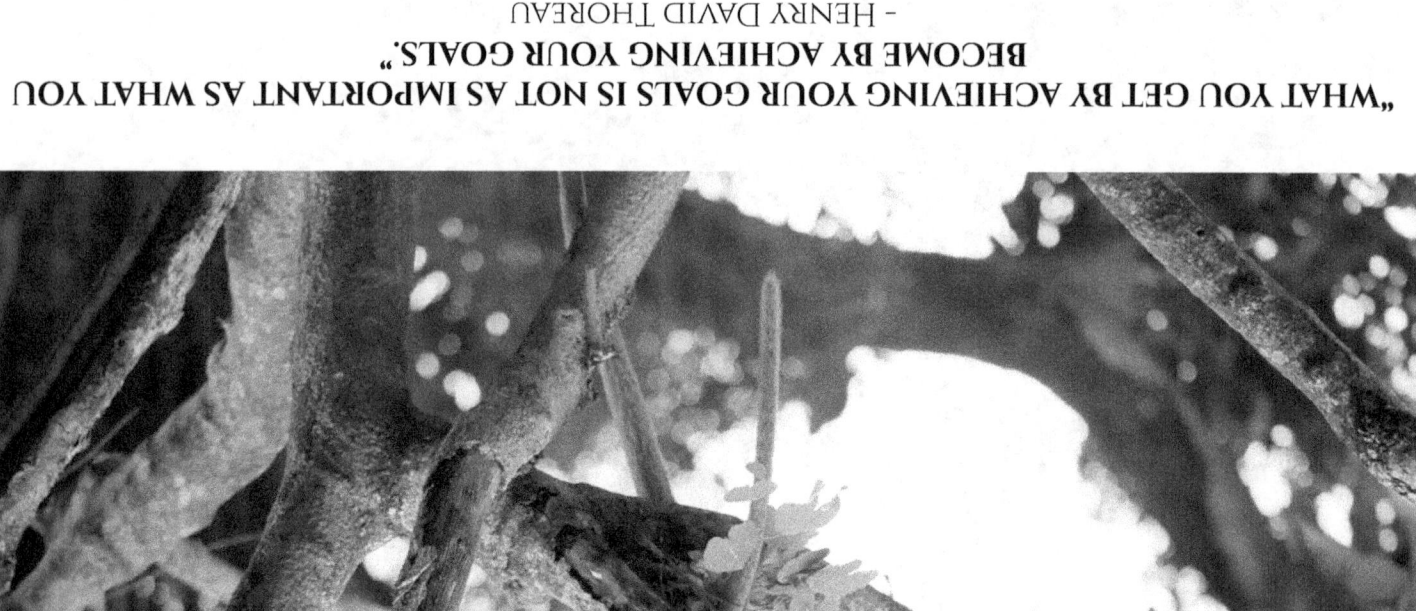

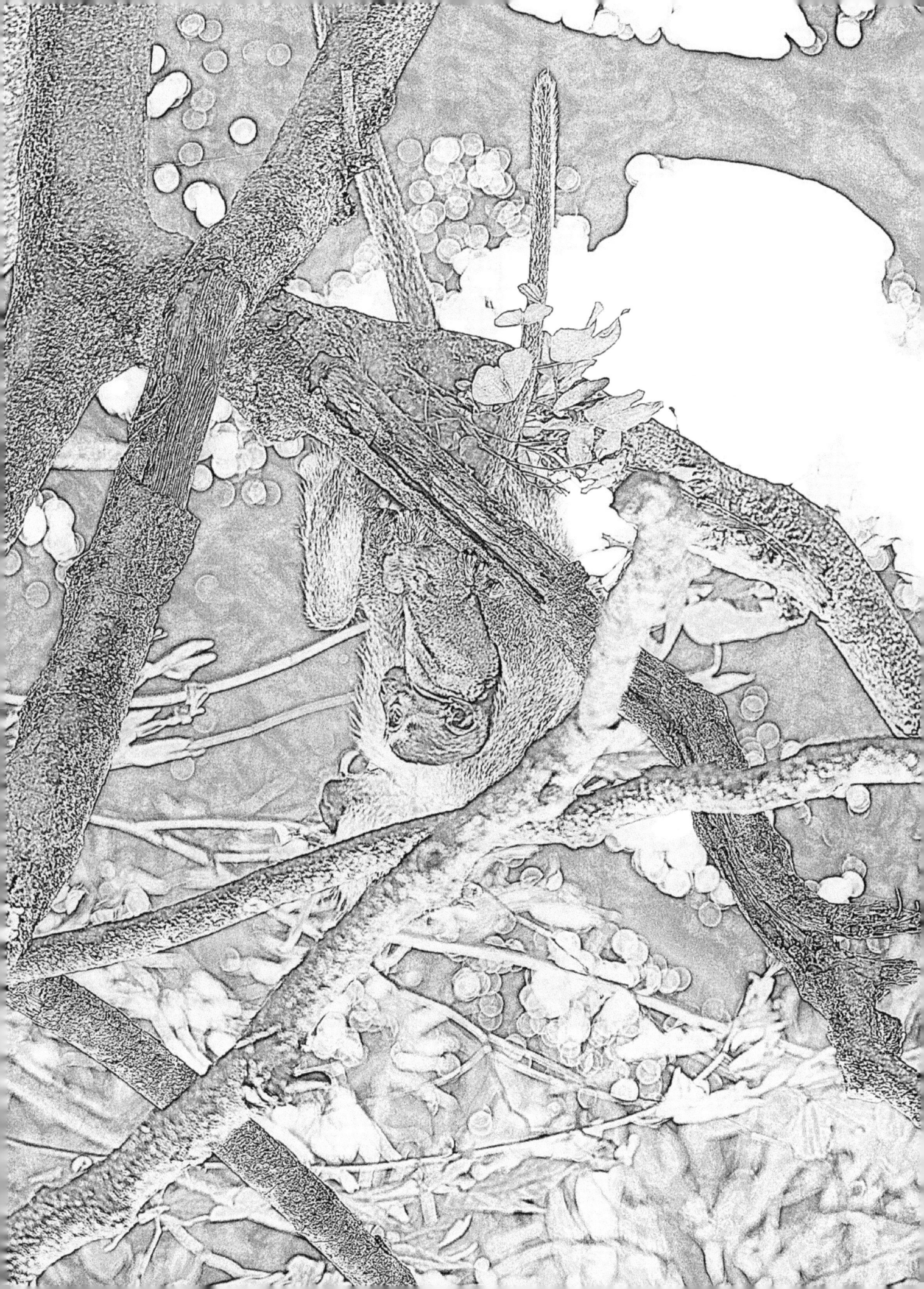

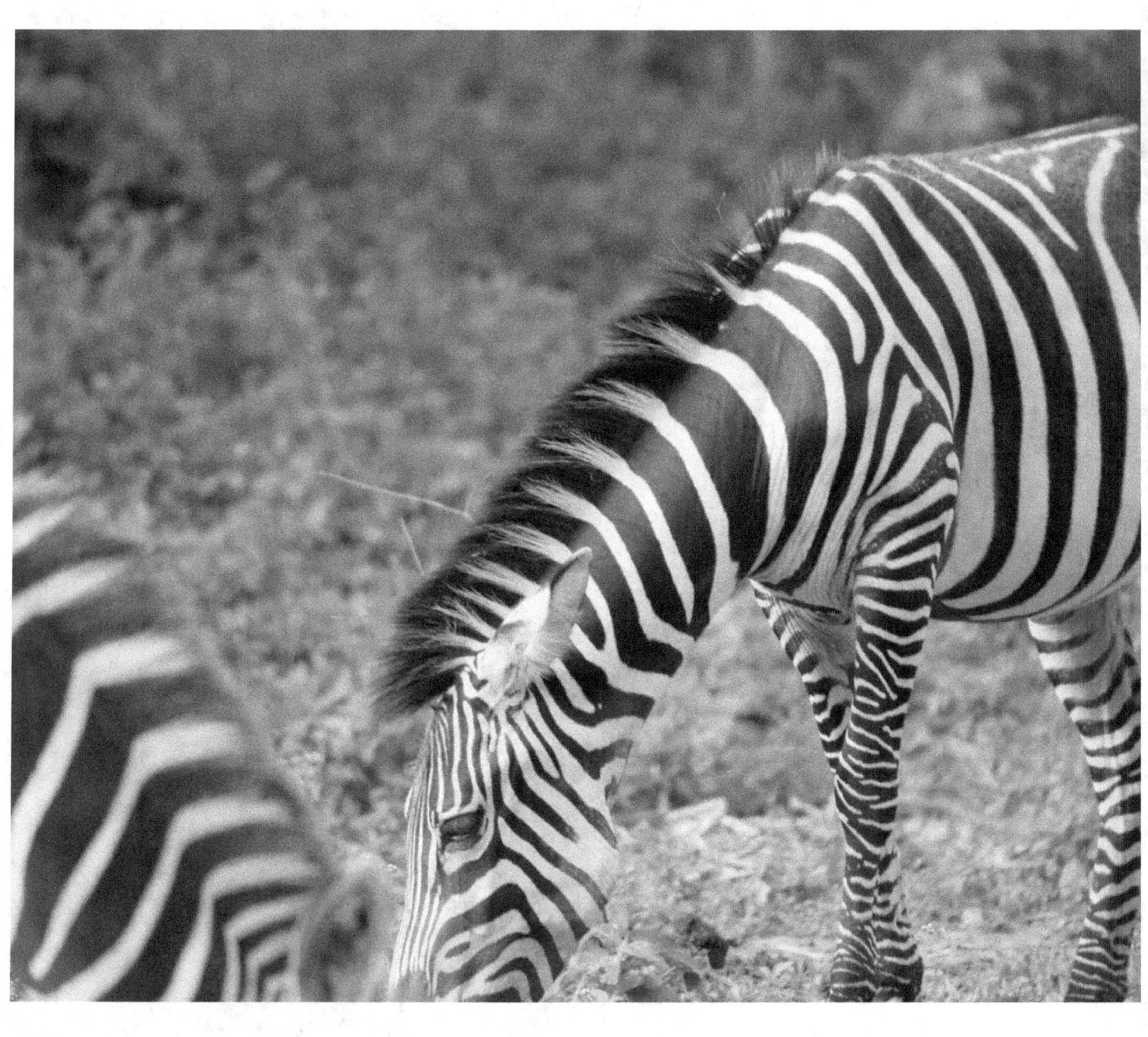

"IF THE PLAN DOESN'T WORK, CHANGE THE PLAN, BUT NEVER THE GOAL."
- AUTHOR UNKNOWN

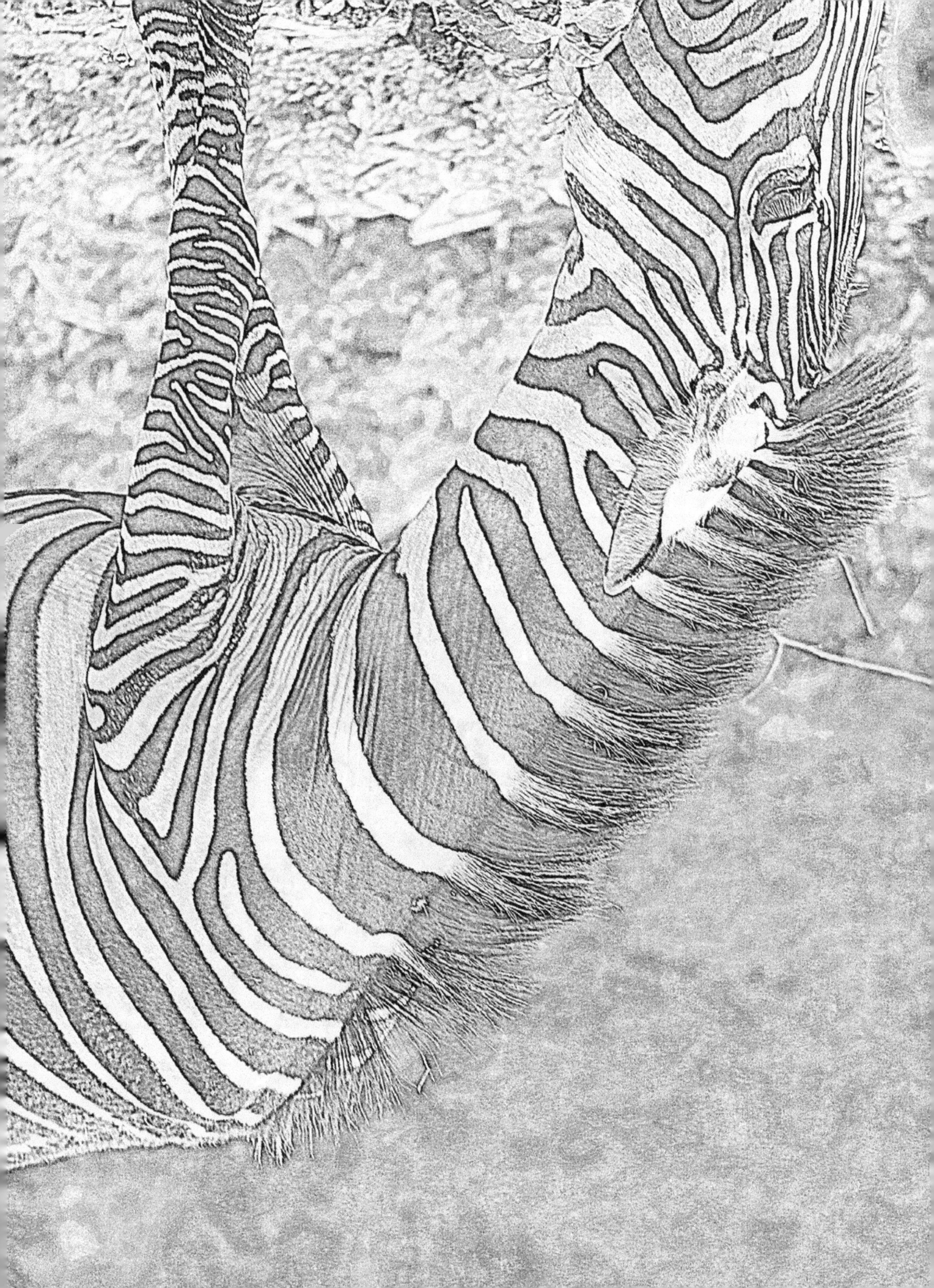

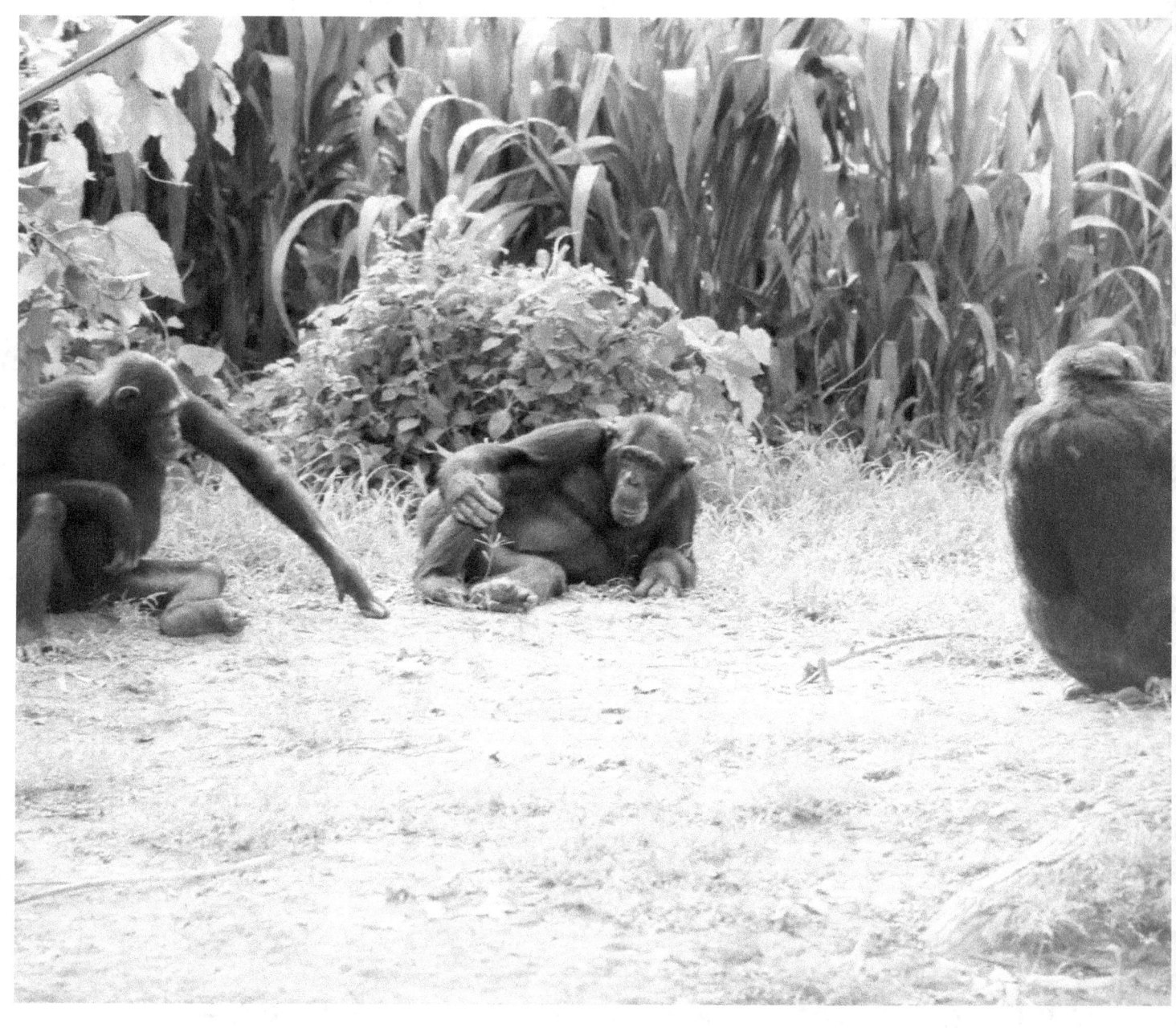

"I DESTROY MY ENEMIES WHEN I MAKE THEM MY FRIENDS."
- ABRAHAM LINCOLN

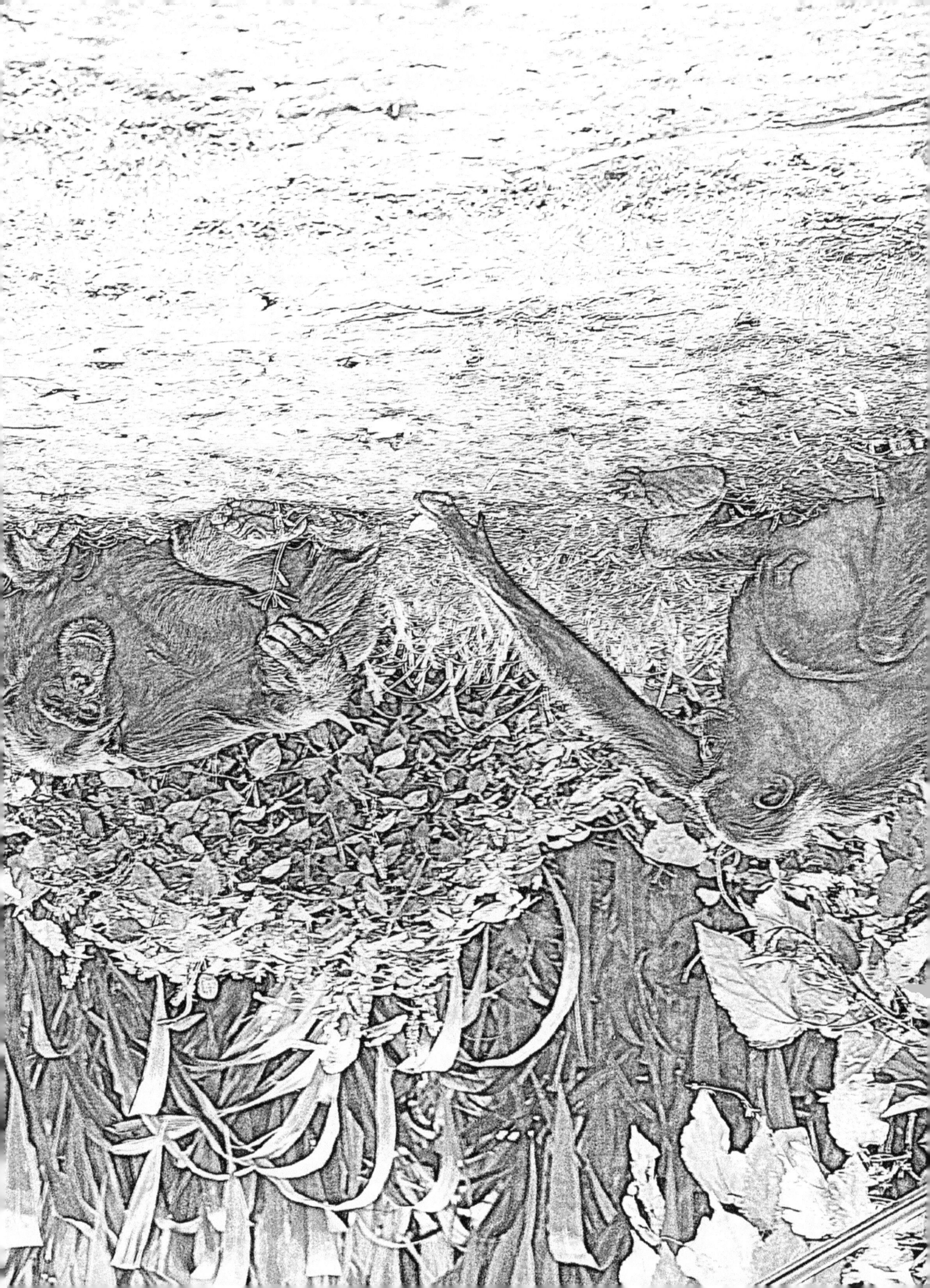

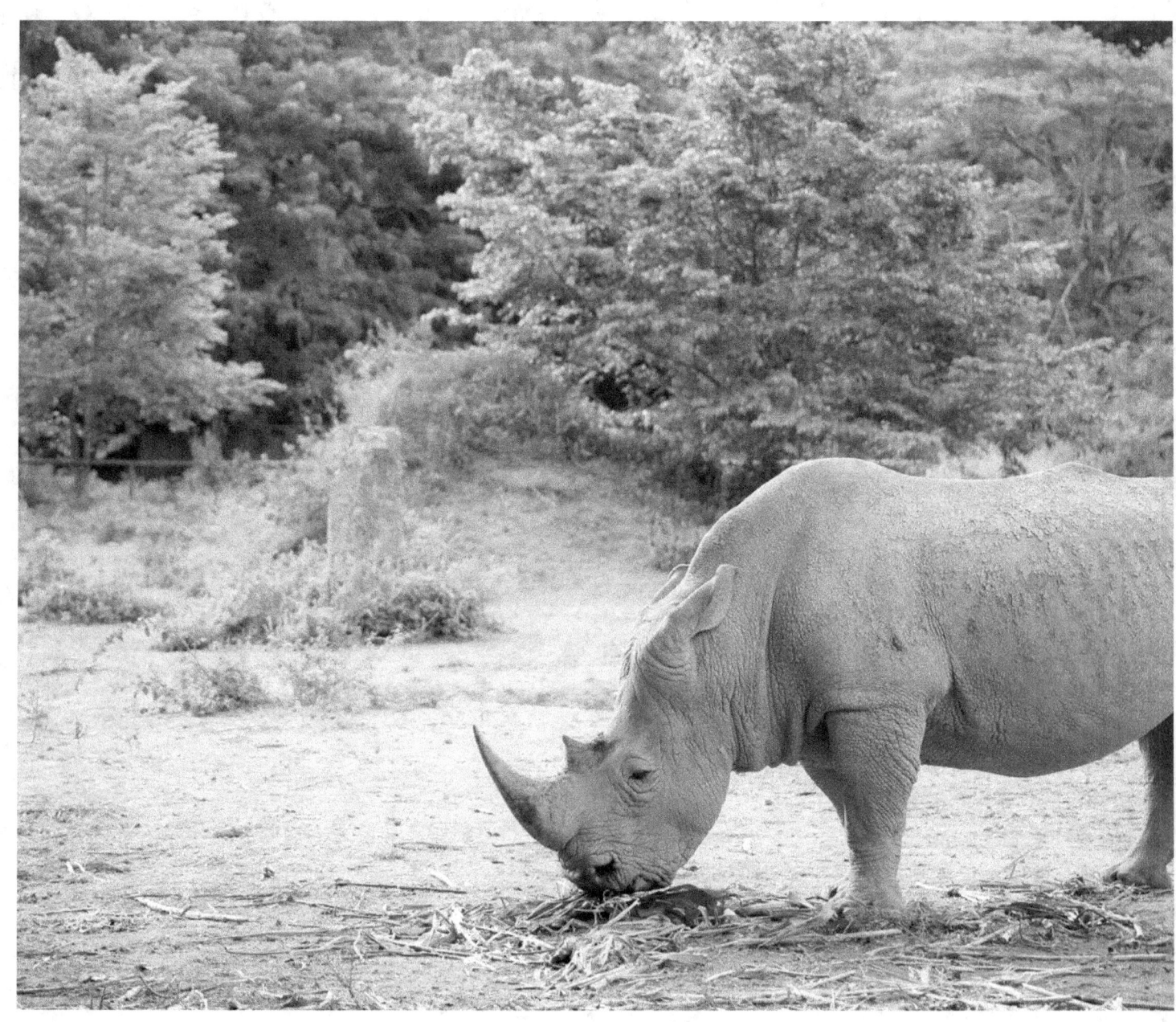

"IT WASN'T RAINING WHEN NOAH BUILT THE ARK."
- HOWARD RUFF

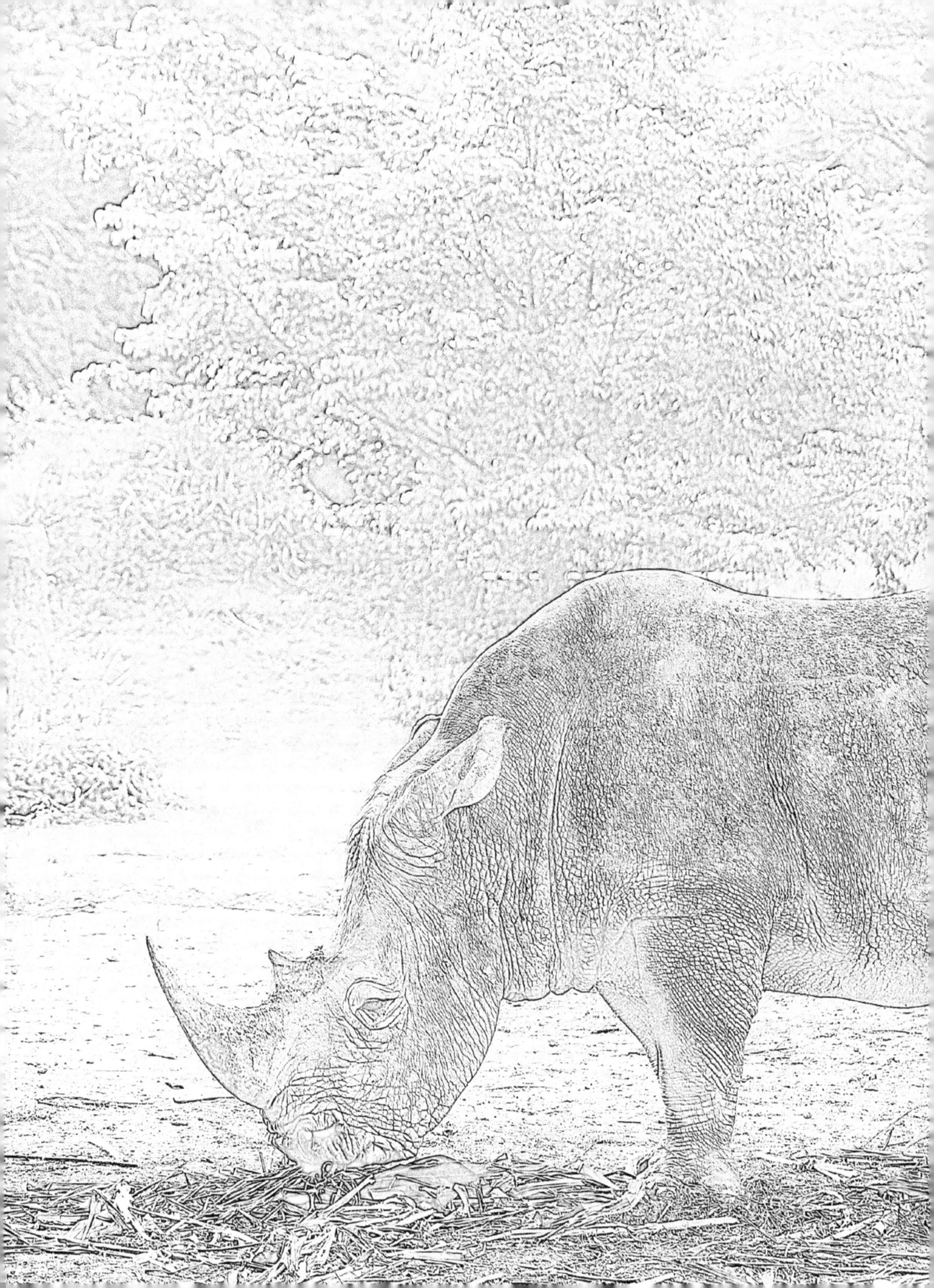

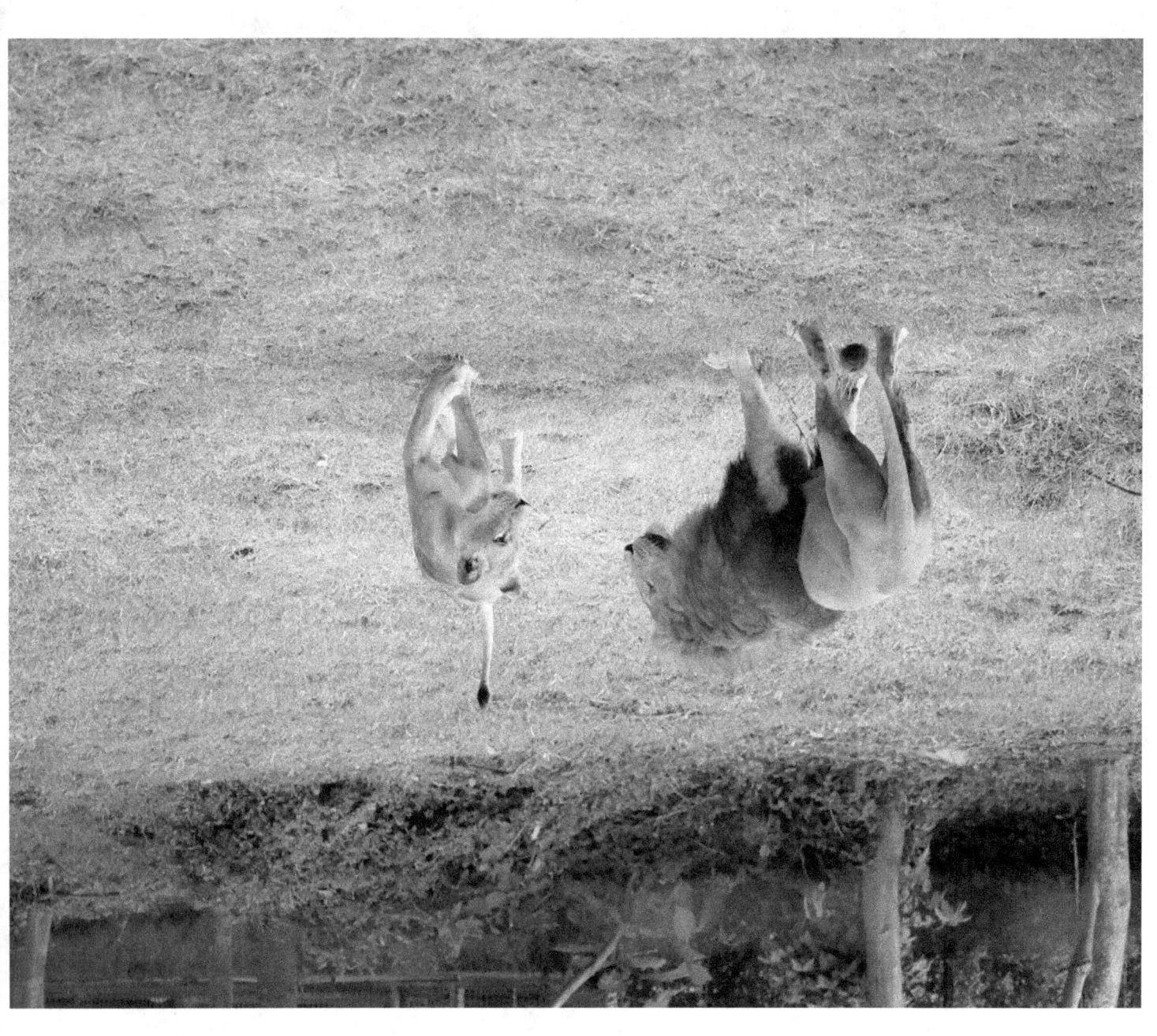

"YOU MUST BE THE CHANGE YOU WISH TO SEE IN THE WORLD."

–MAHATMA GANDHI

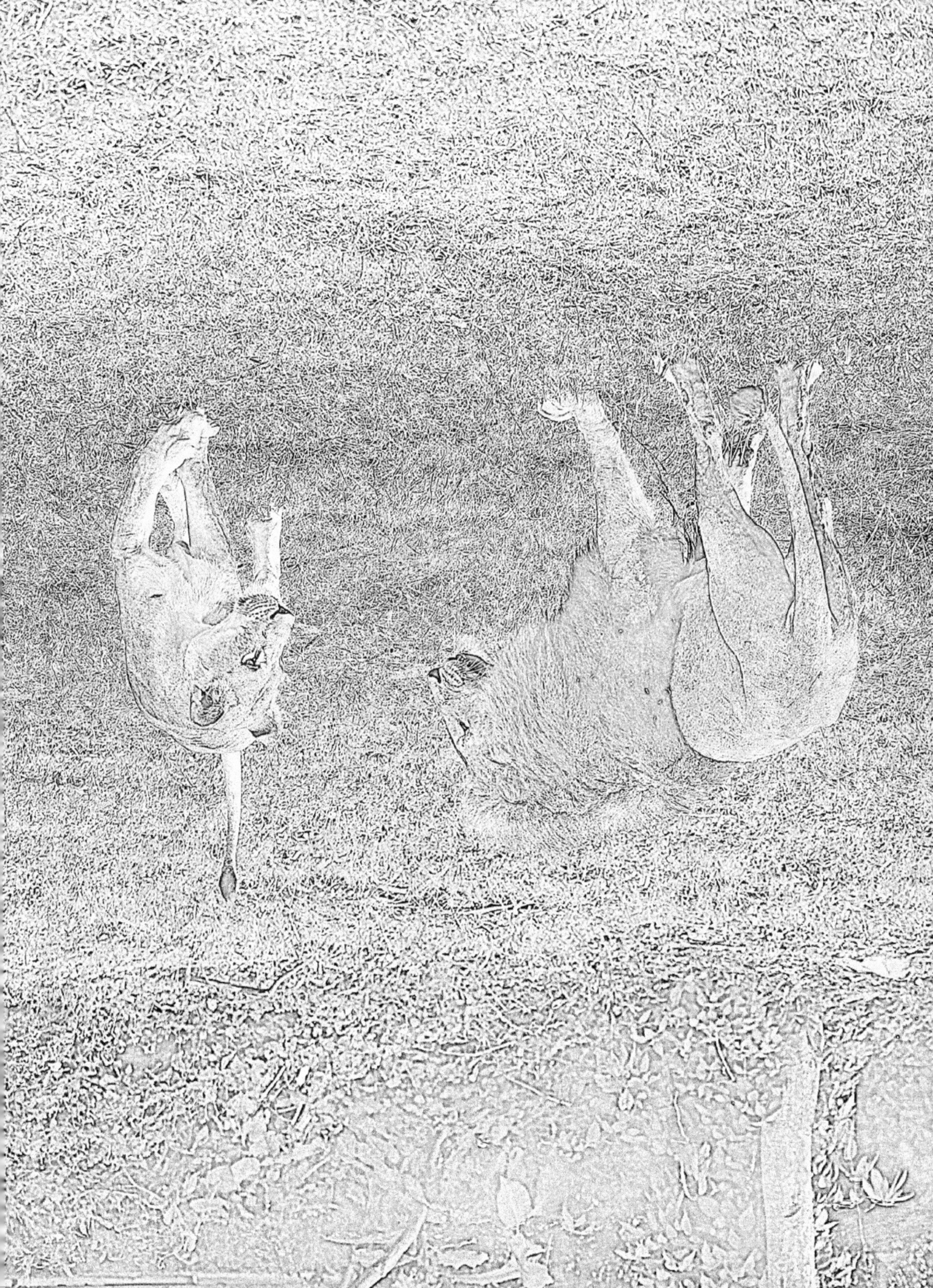

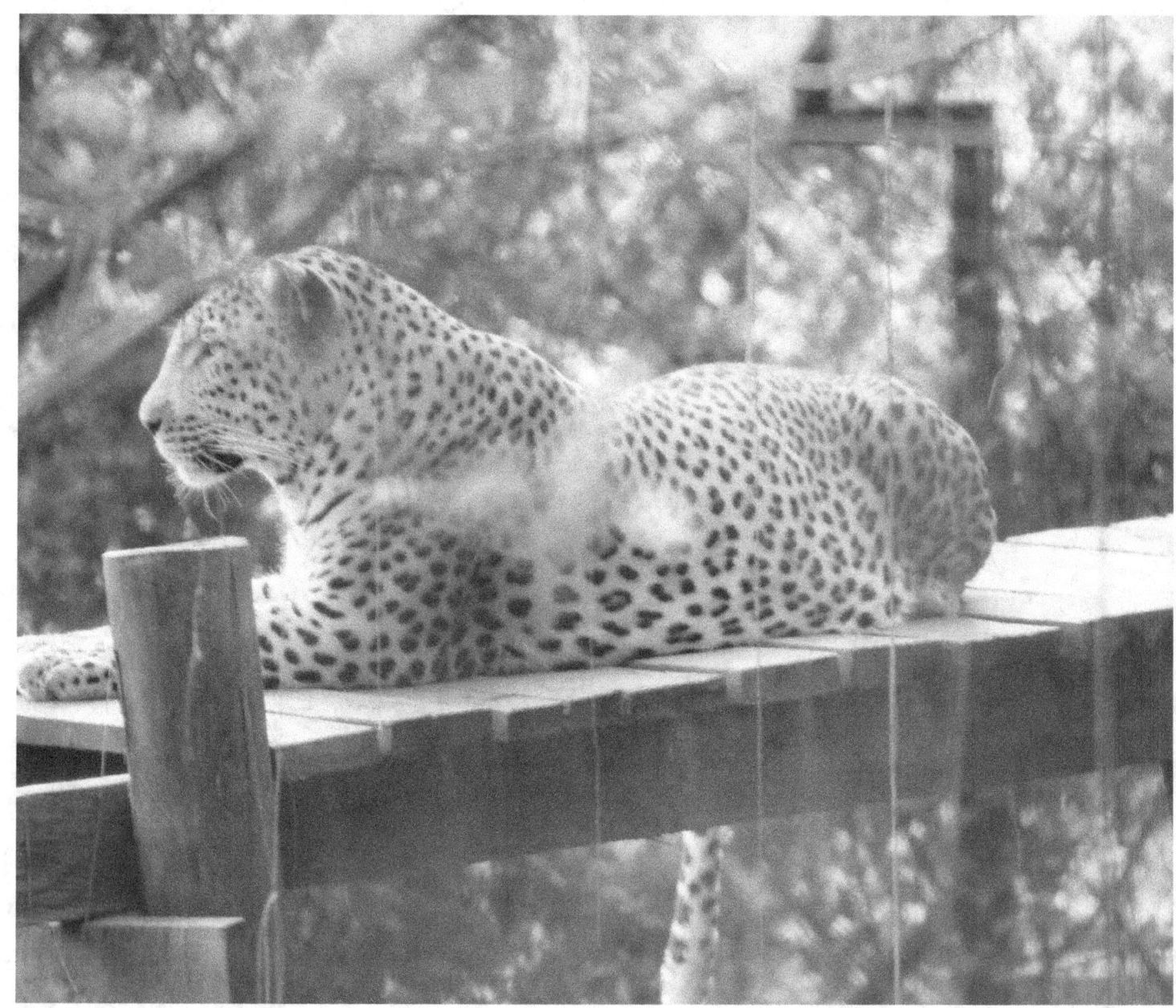

"IF YOU WANT TO LIVE A HAPPY LIFE, TIE IT TO A GOAL, NOT TO PEOPLE OR OBJECTS."
- ALBERT EINSTEIN

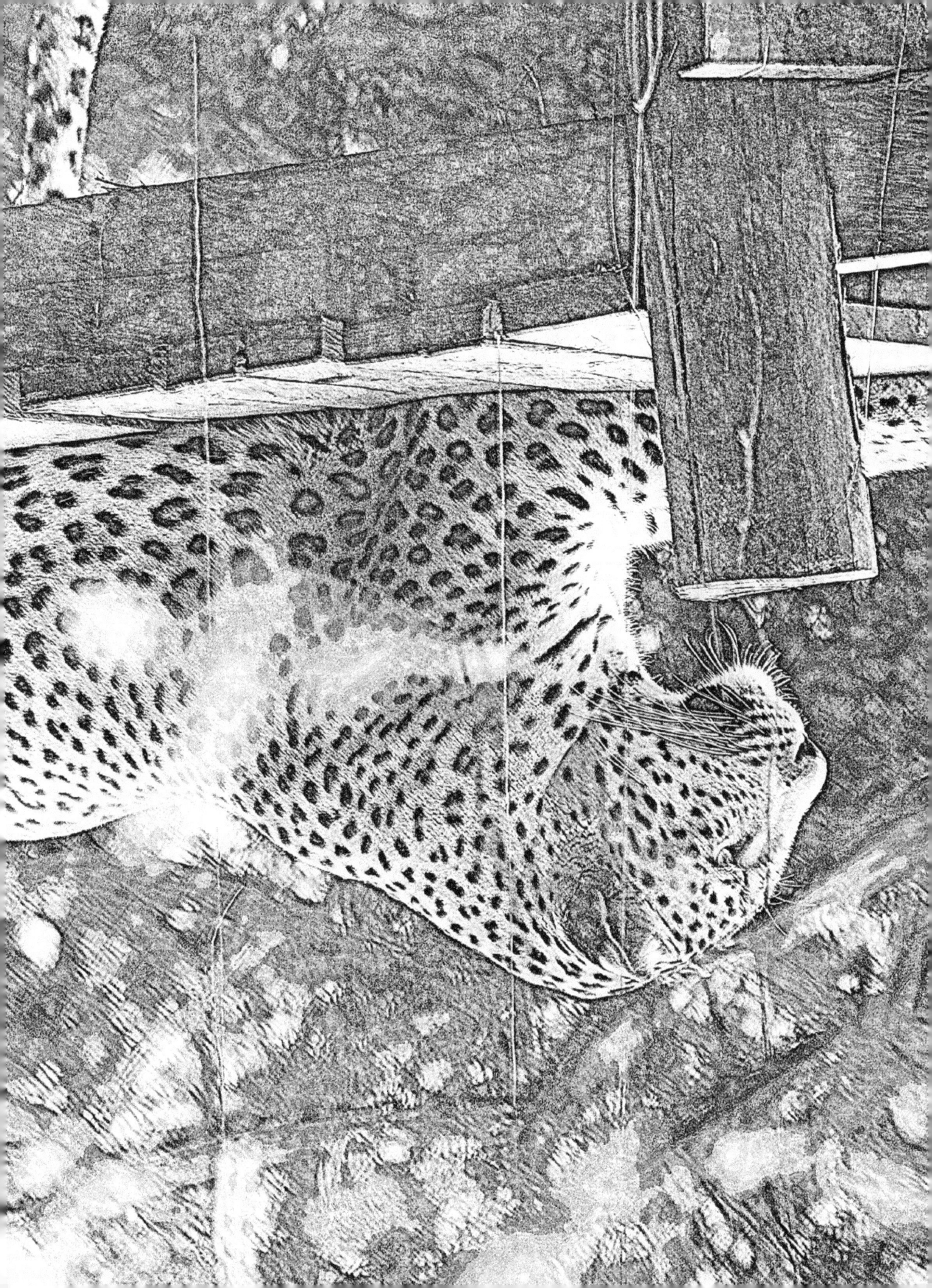

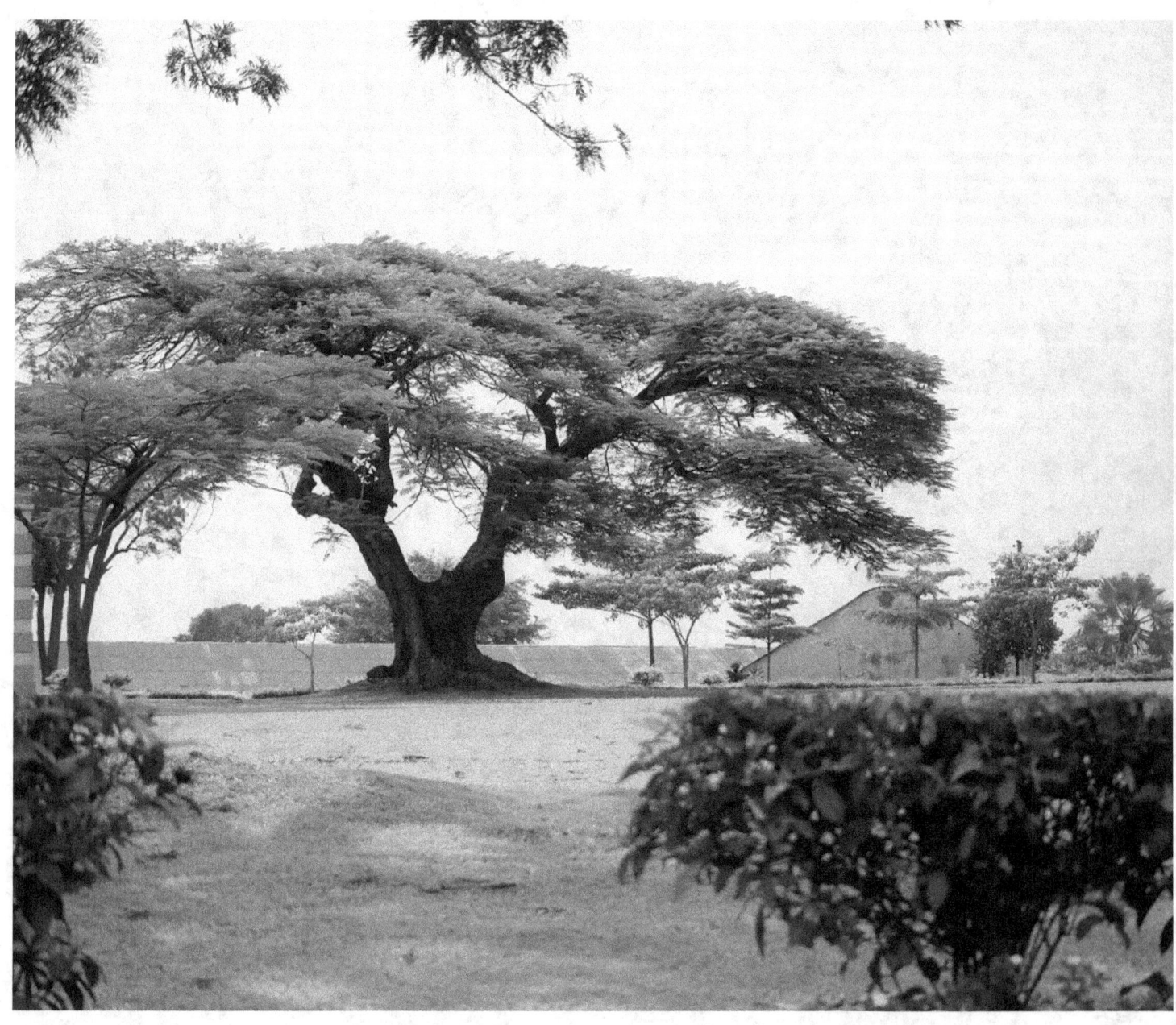

"SOMETIMES YOU WIN, SOMETIMES YOU LEARN."
- JOHN MAXWELL

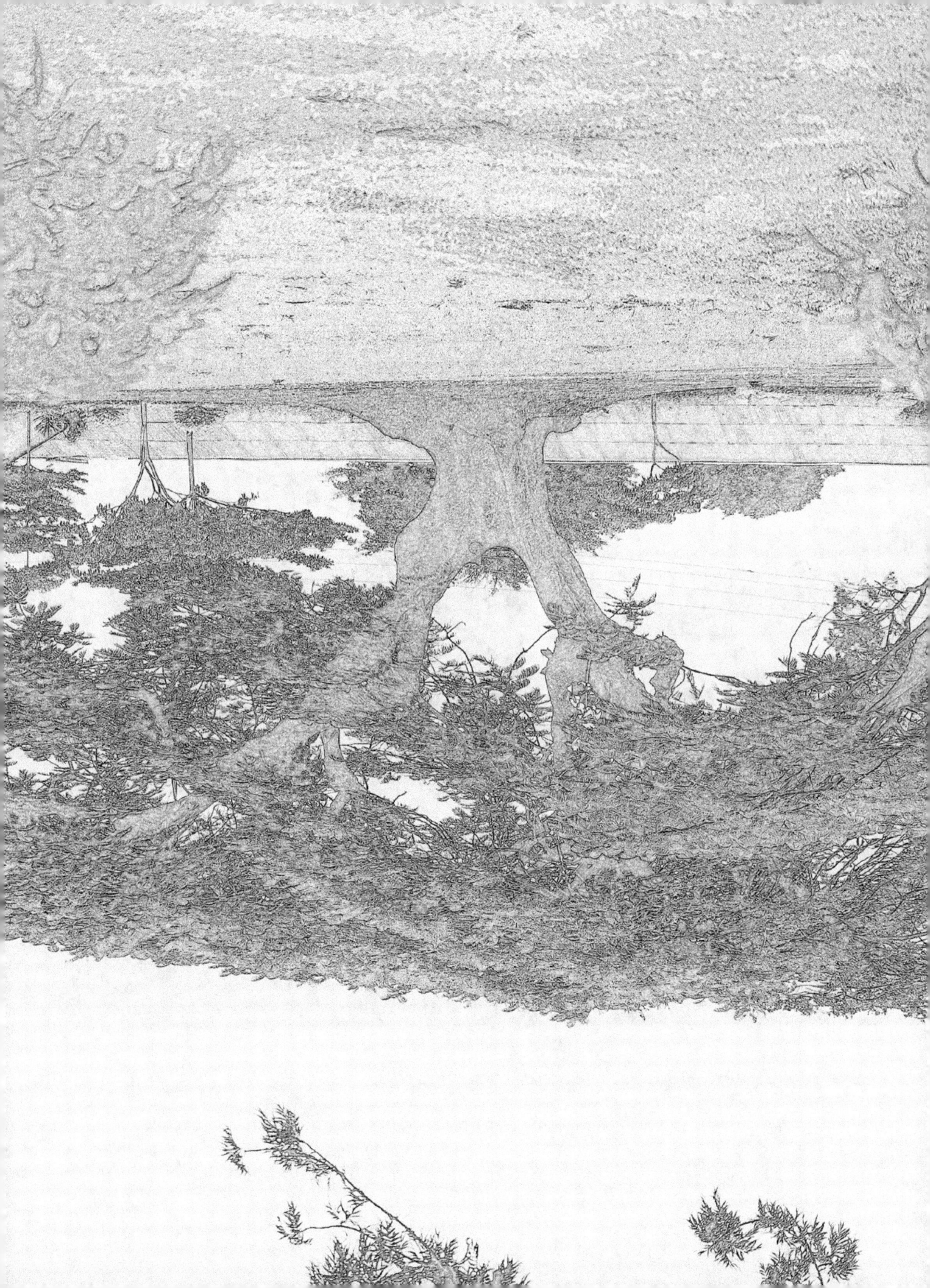

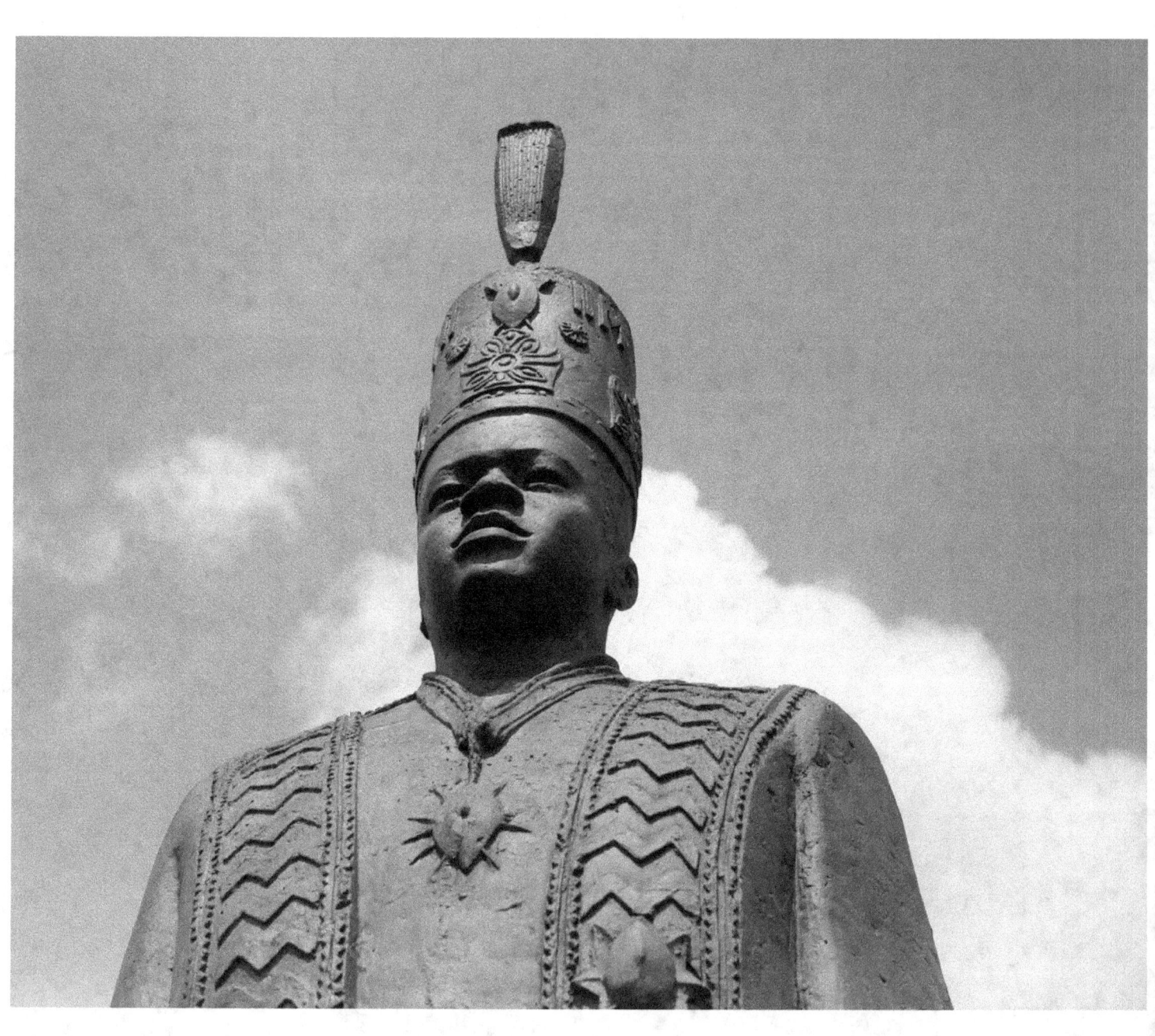

"BUT MAN IS NOT MADE FOR DEFEAT. A MAN CAN BE DESTROYED BUT NOT DEFEATED."
- ERNEST HEMINGWAY

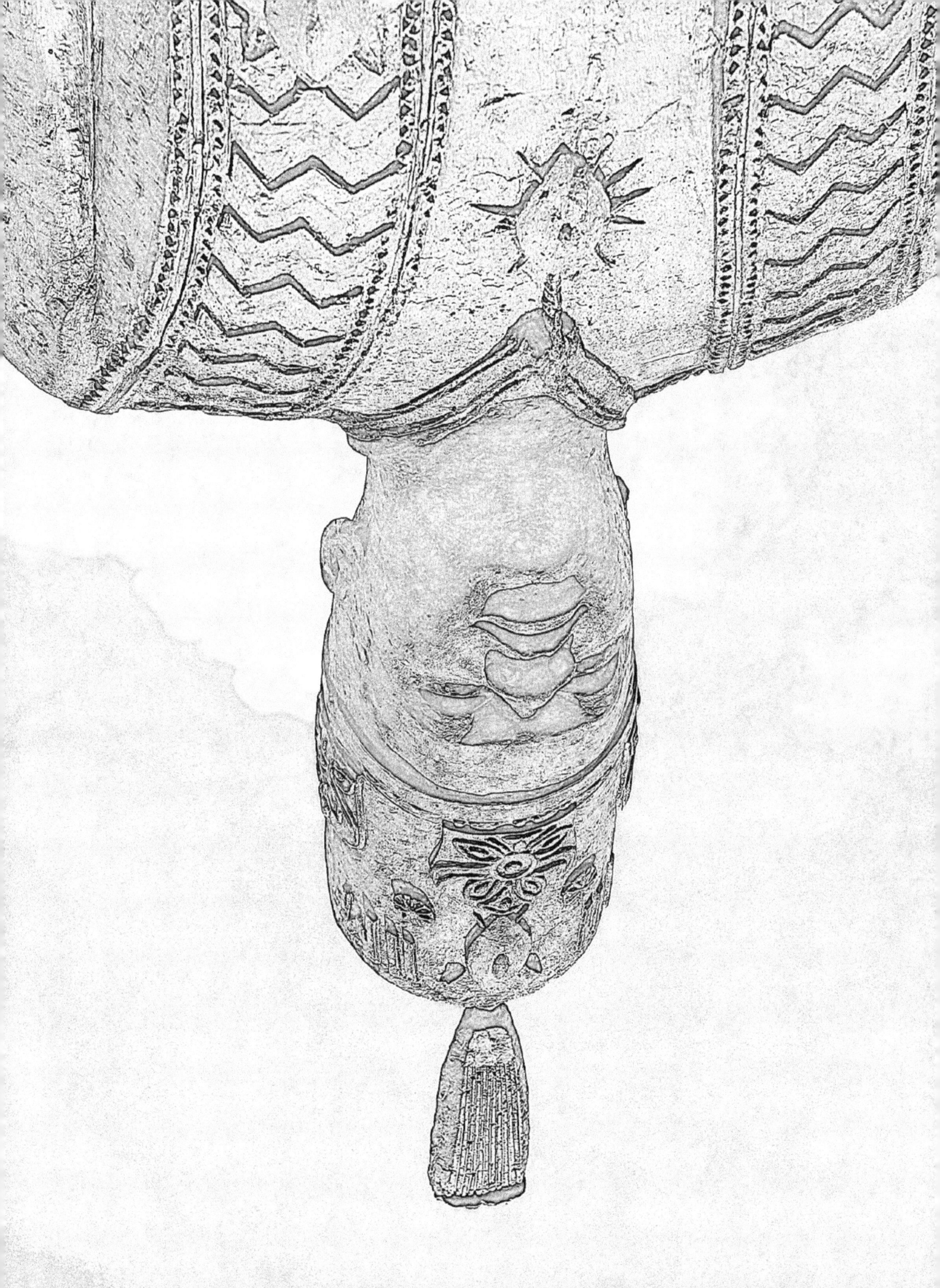

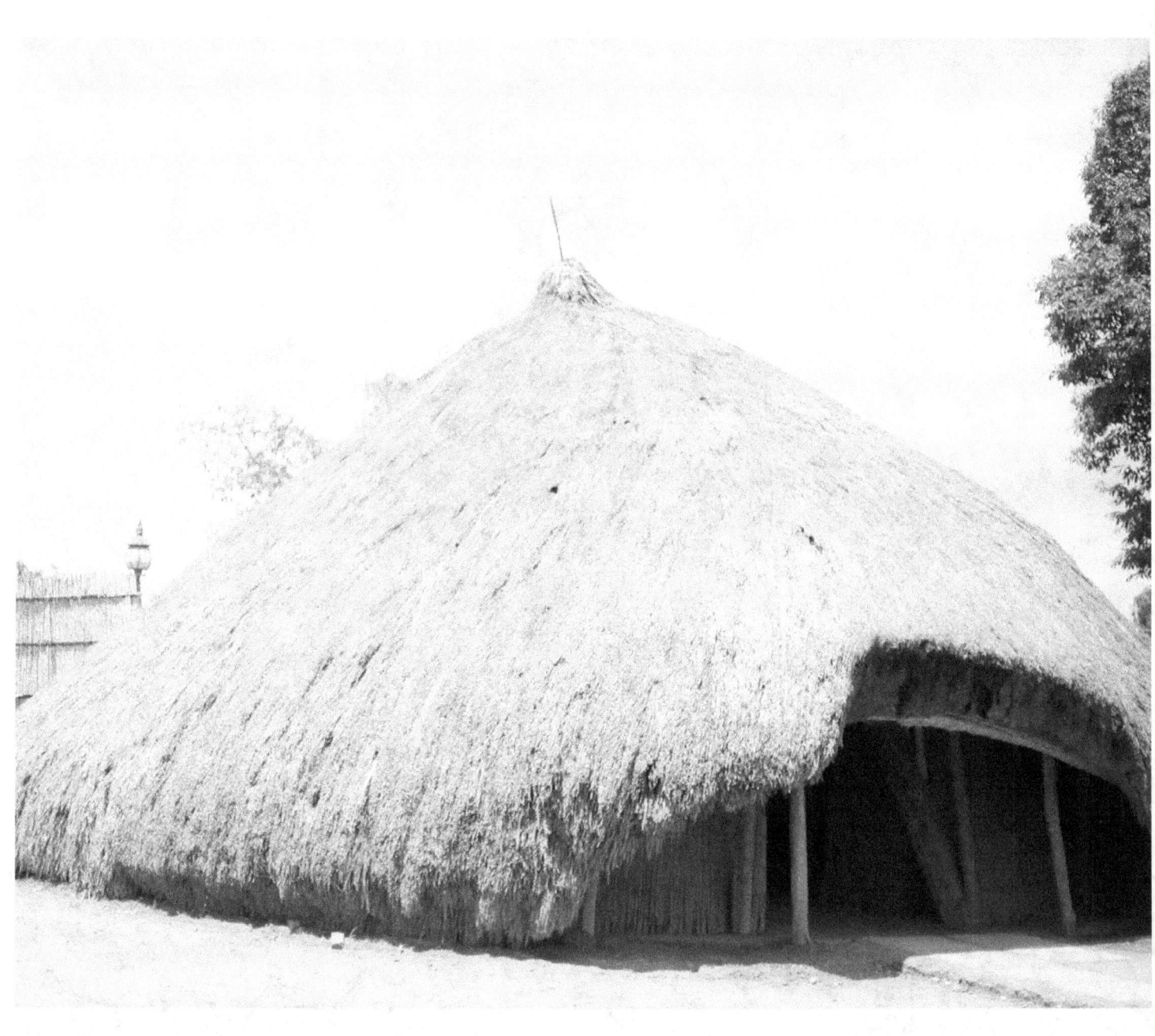

"THERE IS NOTHING PERMANENT EXCEPT CHANGE."
- HERACLITUS

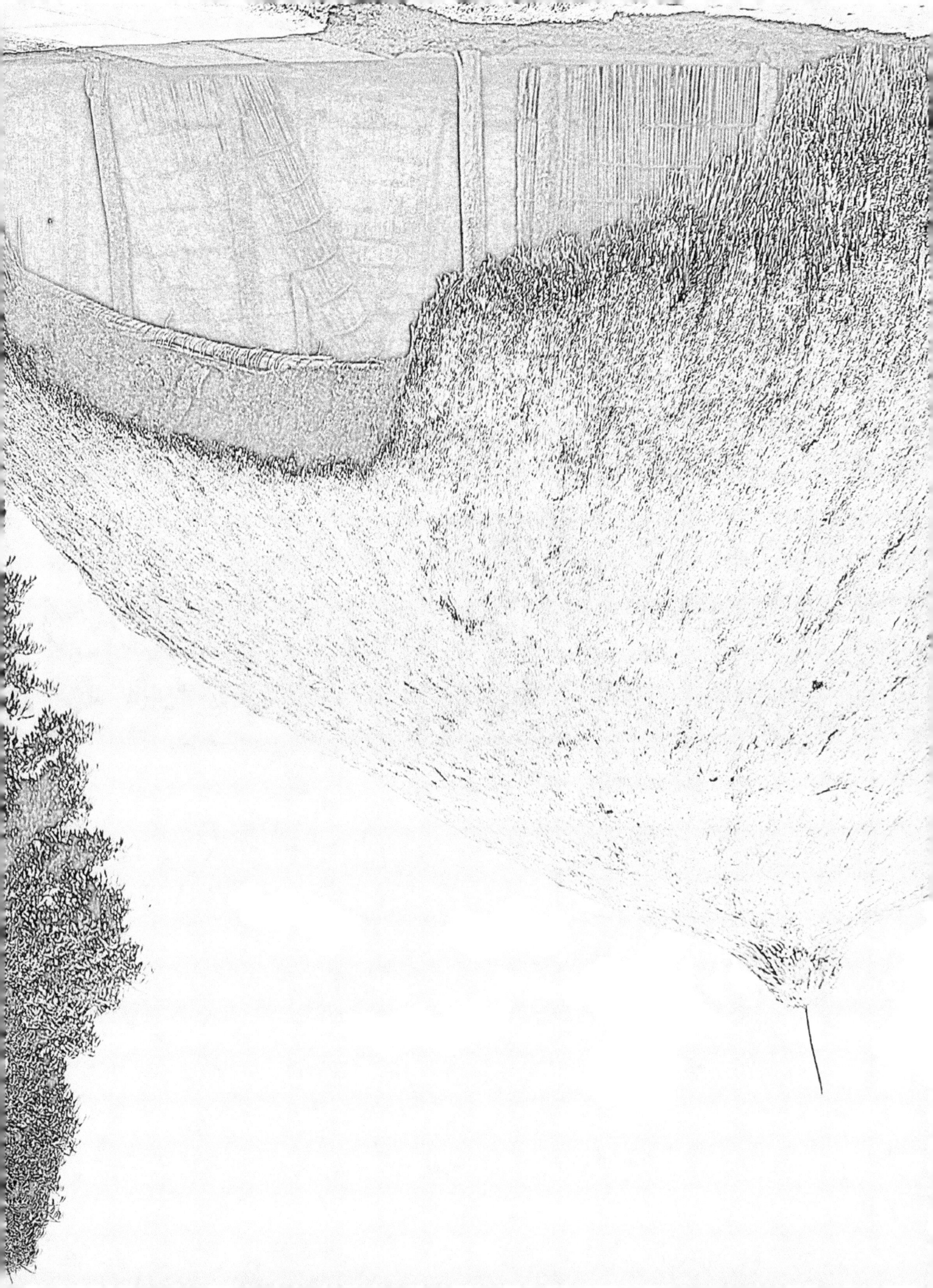

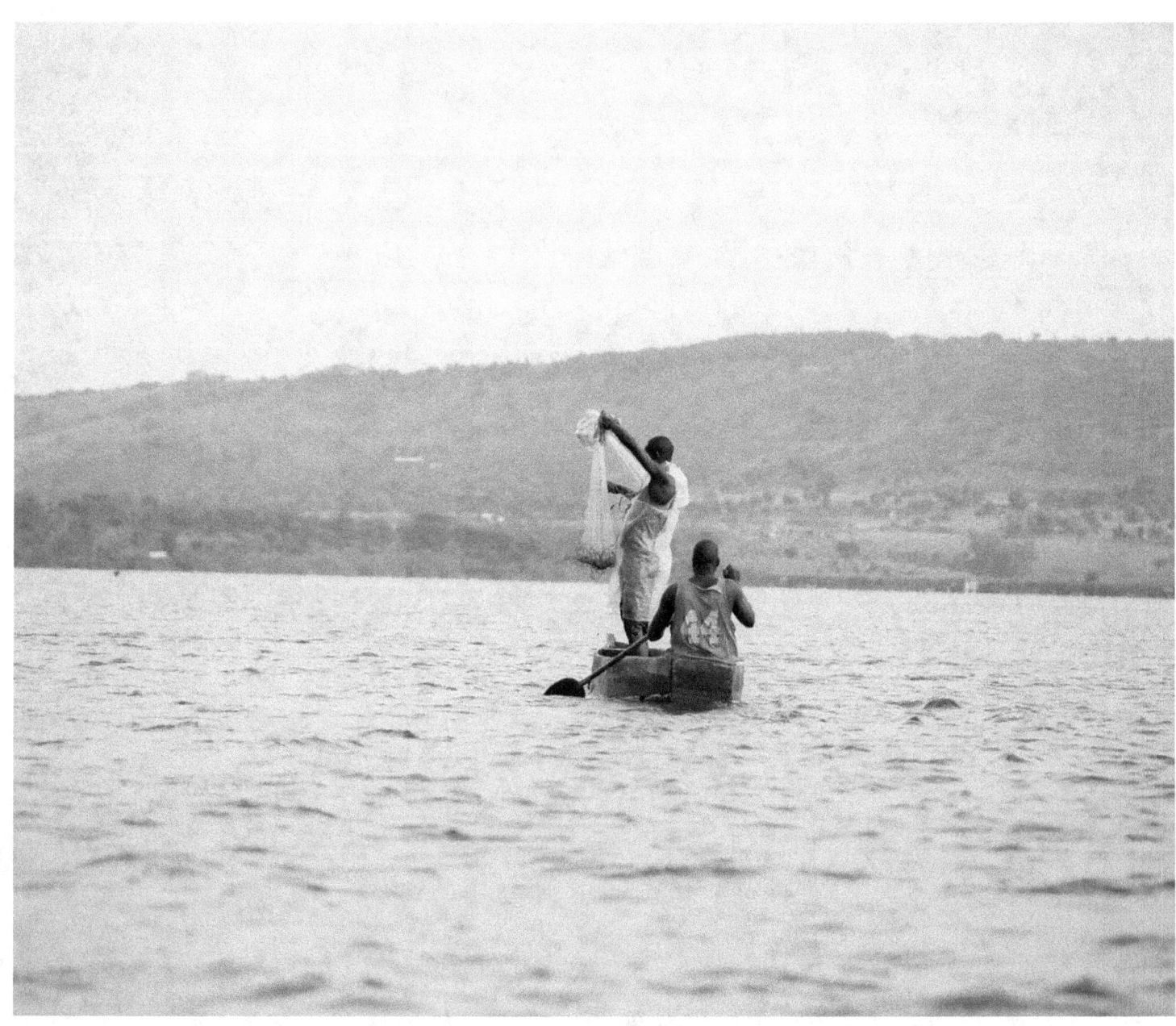

"Learning never exhausts the mind."
- Leonardo da Vinci

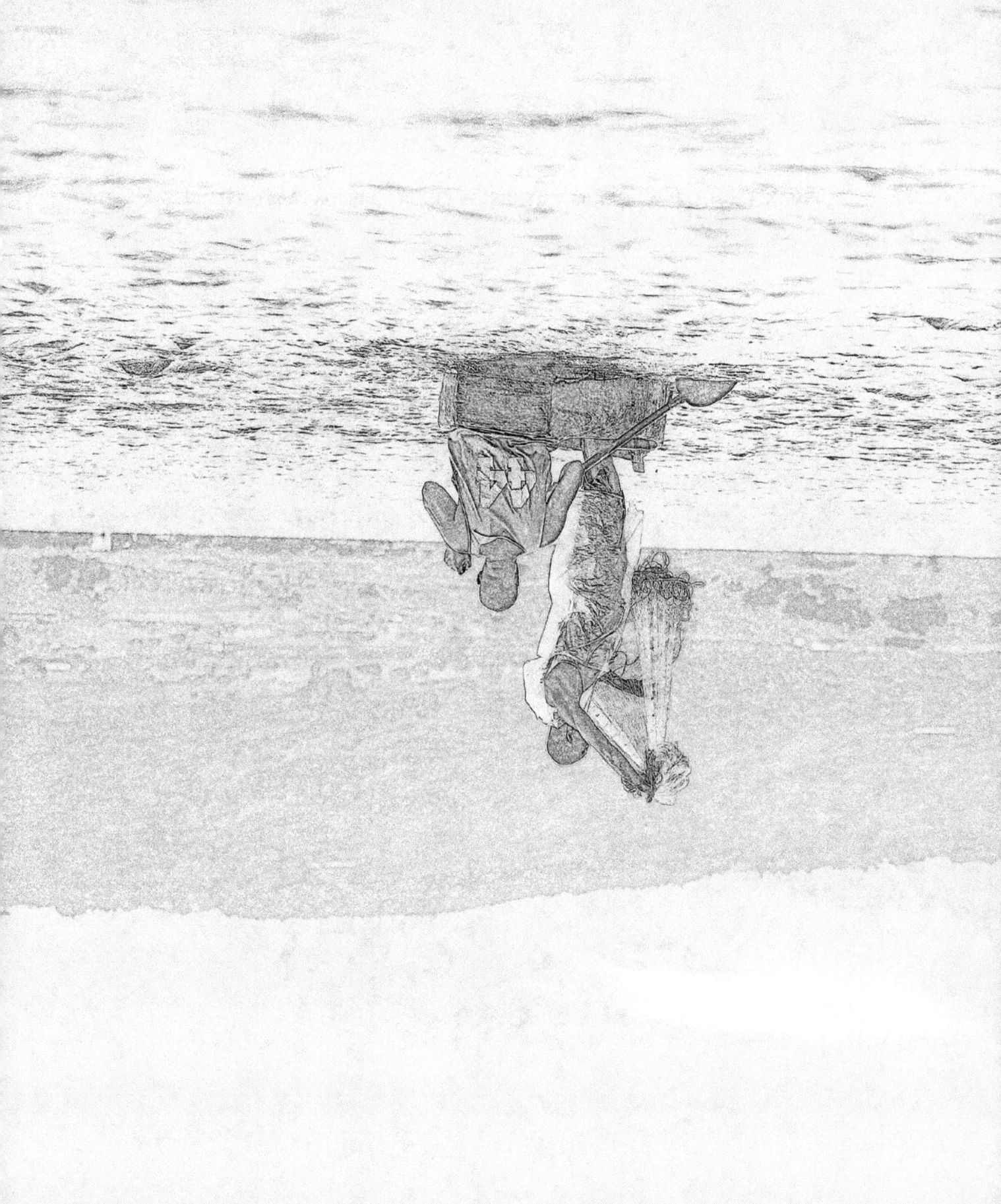

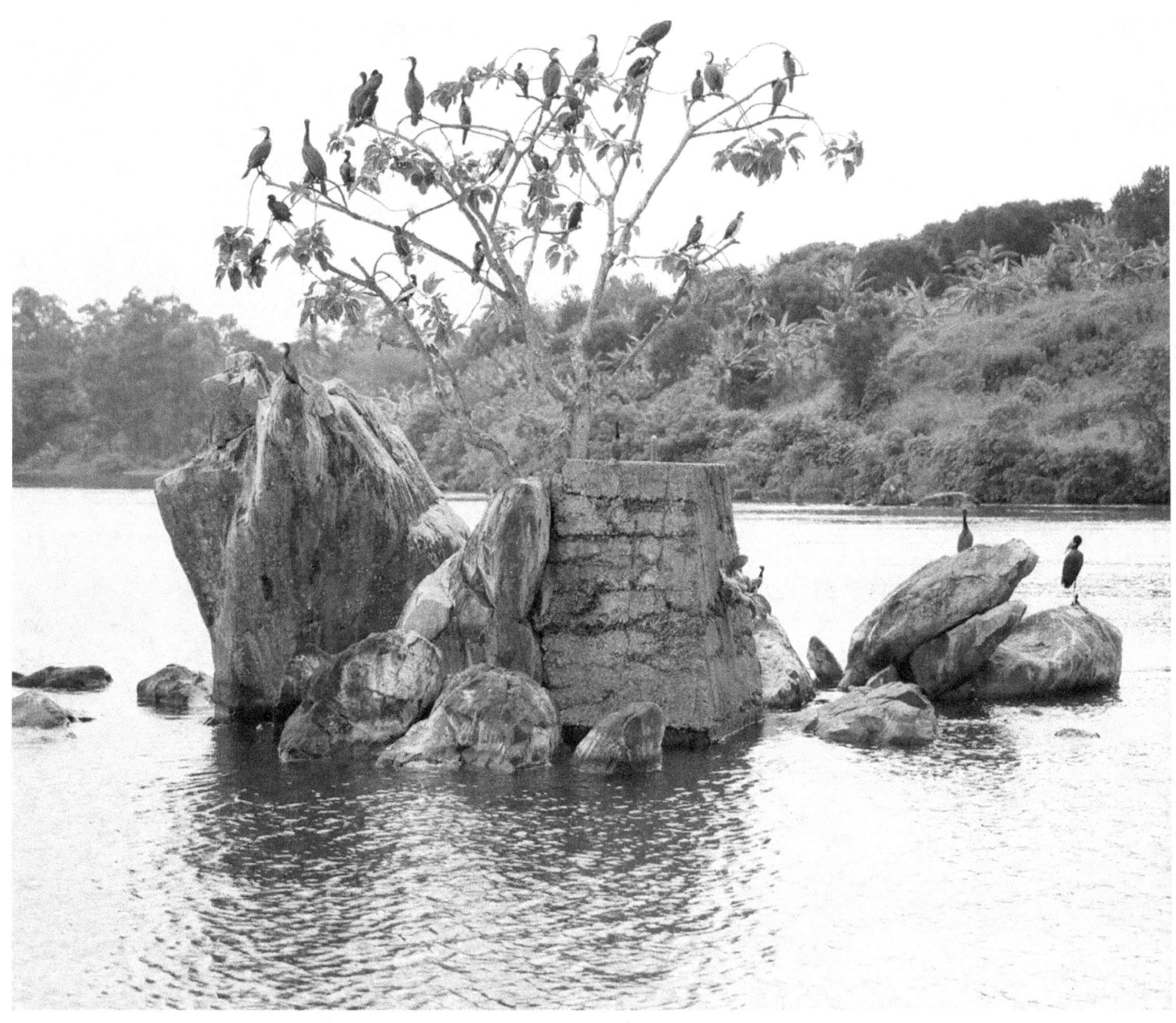

"ALL THAT WE SEE OR SEEM IS BUT A DREAM WITHIN A DREAM."
- EDGAR ALLAN POE

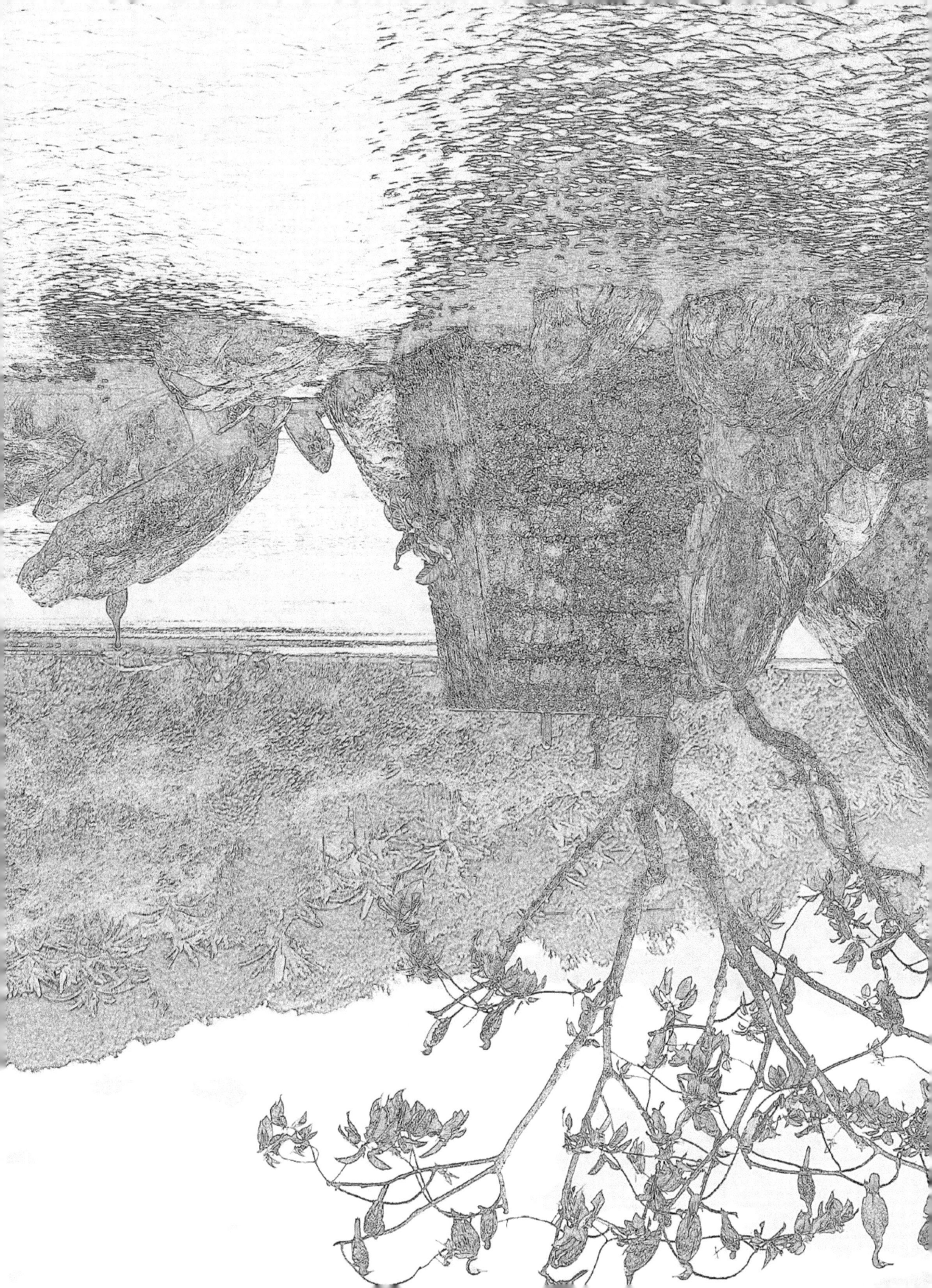

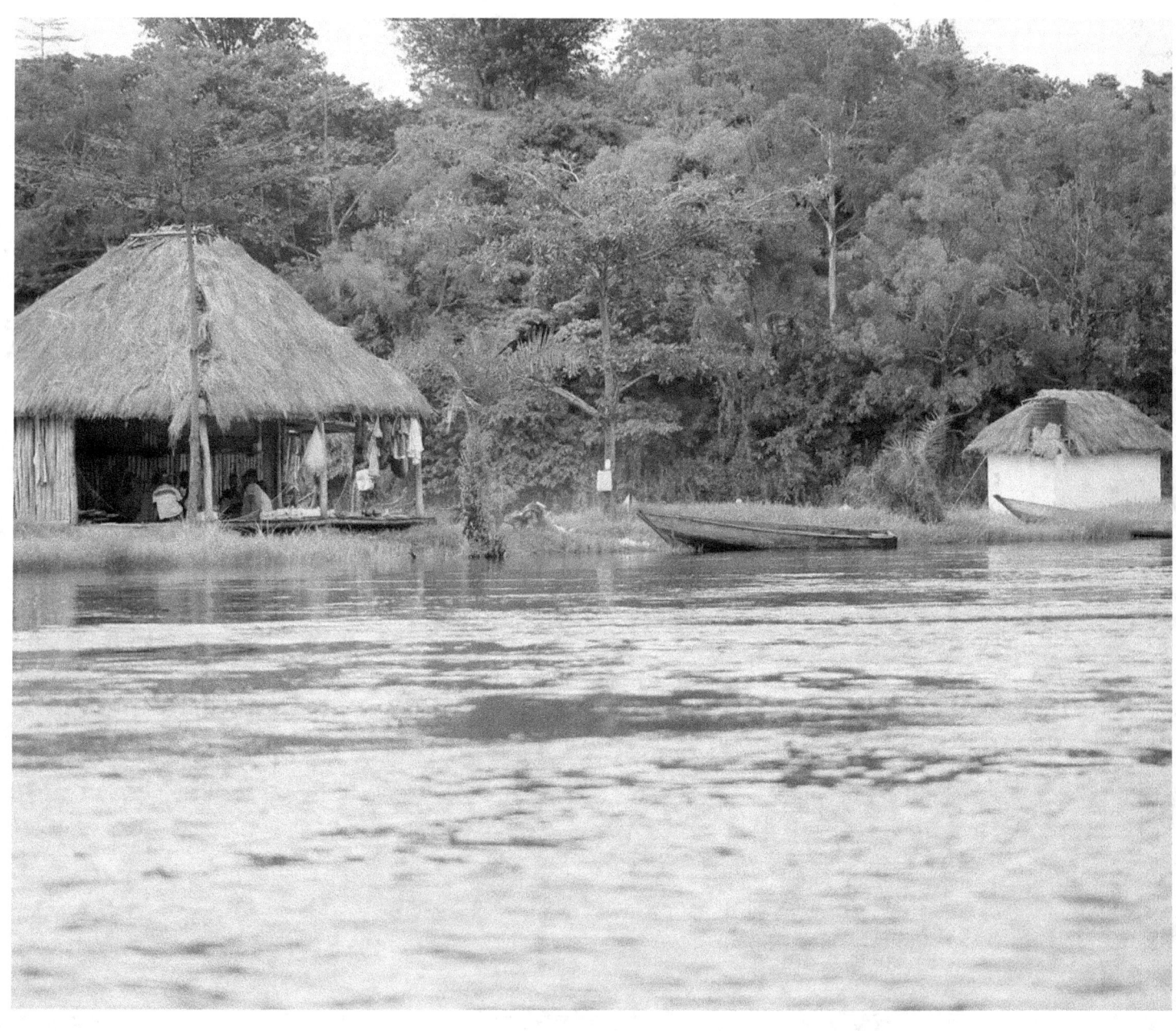

"LORD, MAKE ME AN INSTRUMENT OF THY PEACE.
WHERE THERE IS HATRED, LET ME SOW LOVE."
- FRANCIS OF ASSISI

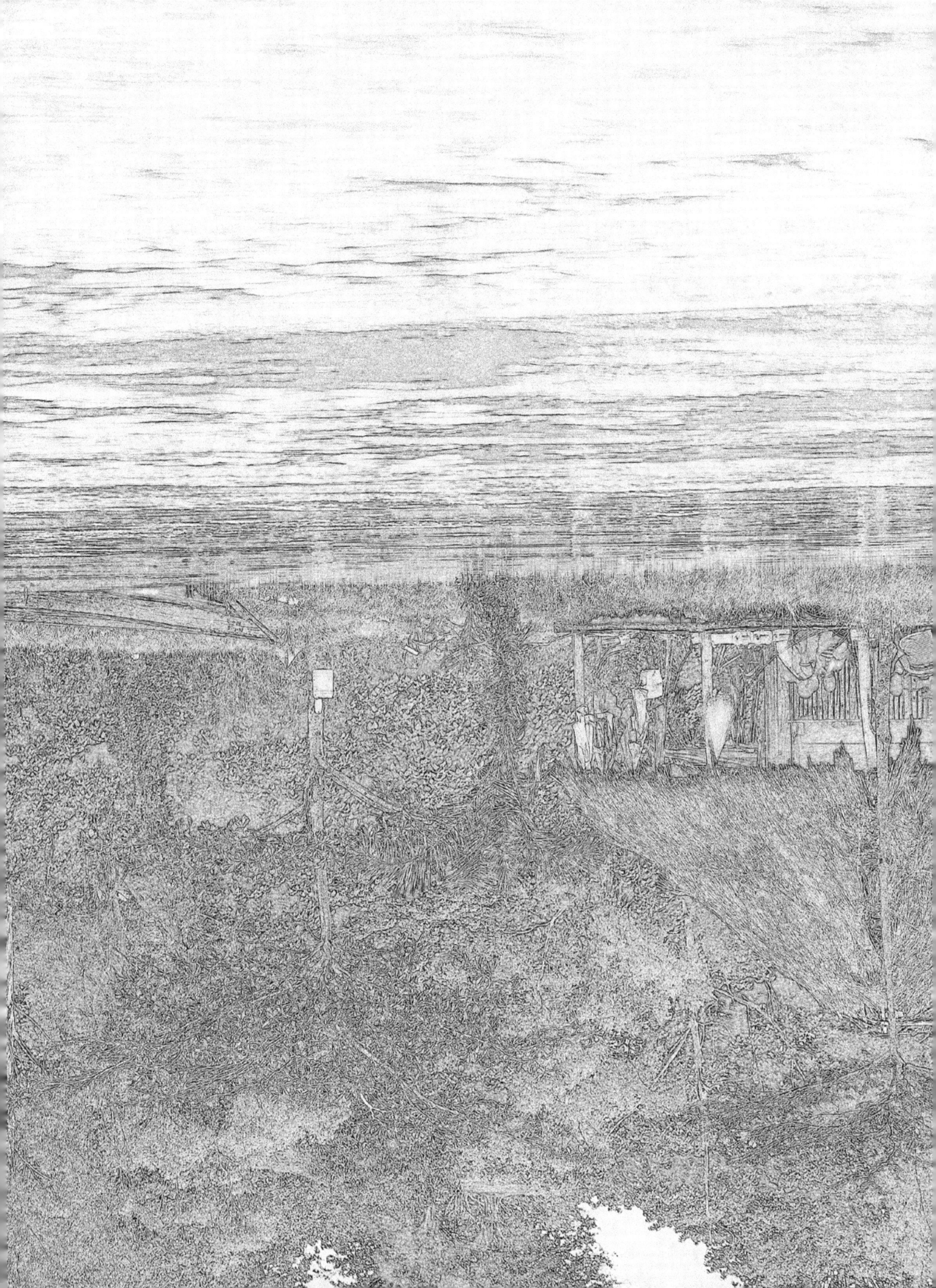

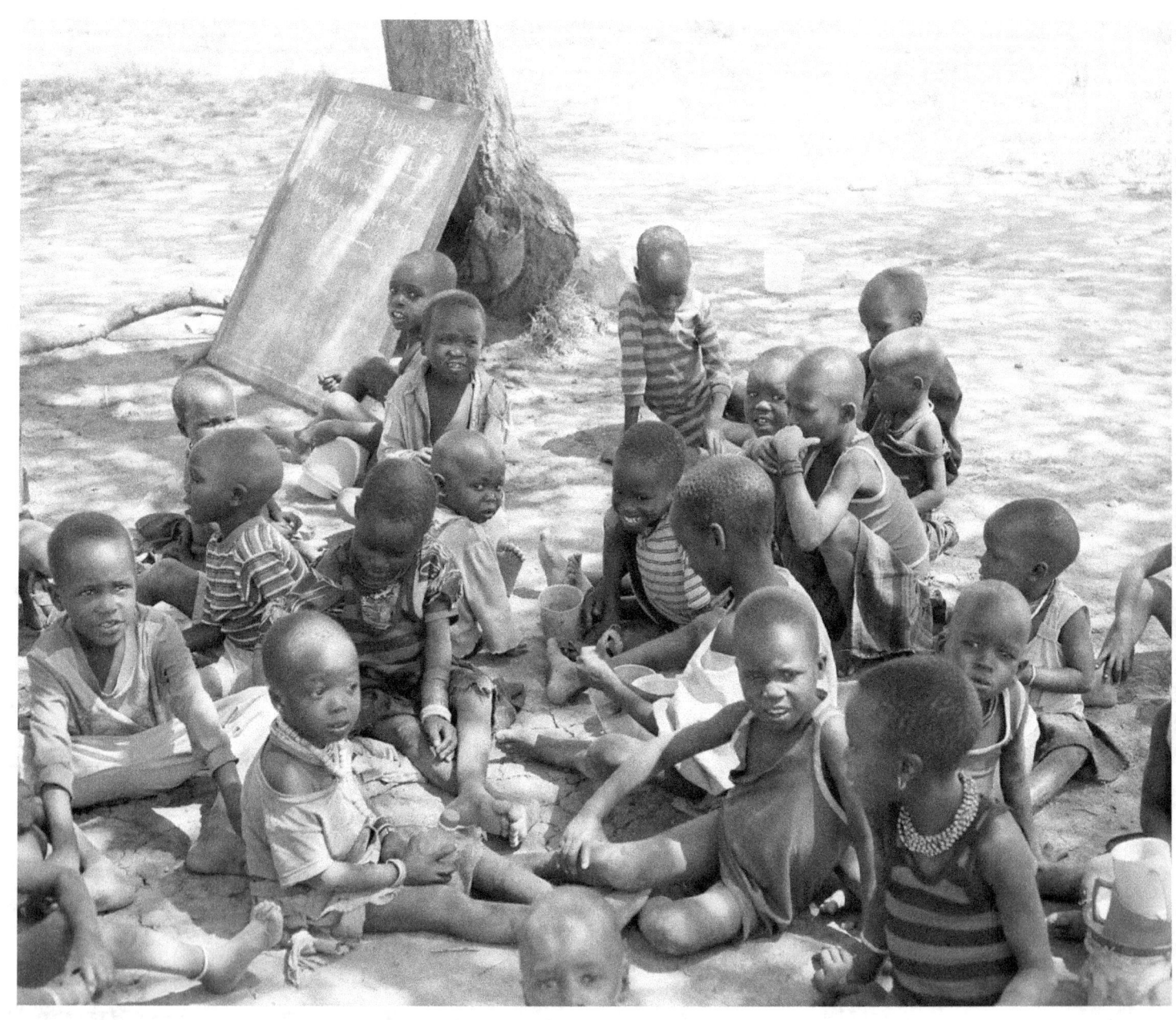

"LOVE CURES PEOPLE – BOTH THE ONES WHO GIVE IT AND THE ONES WHO RECEIVE IT."
- KARL A. MENNINGER

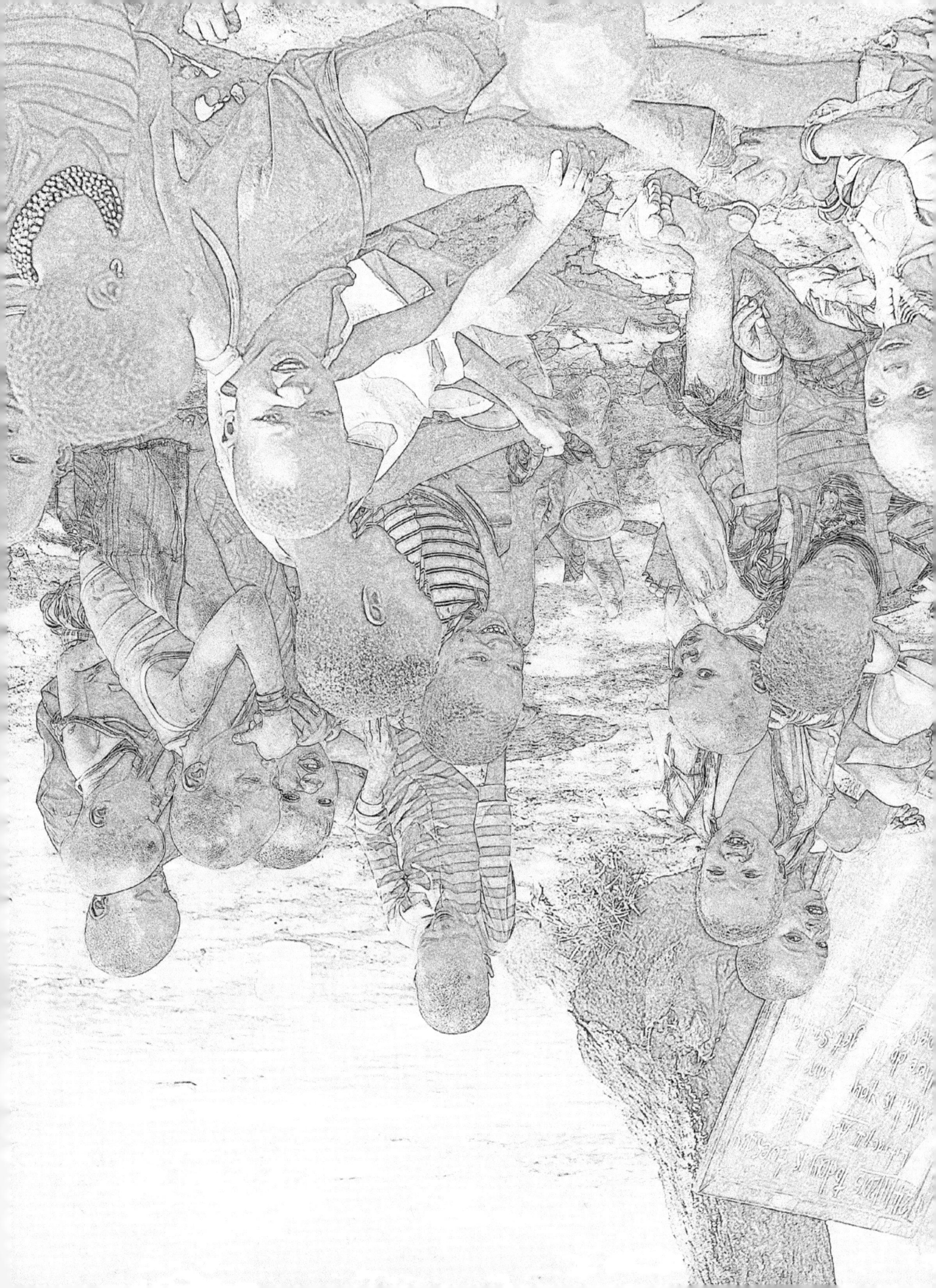

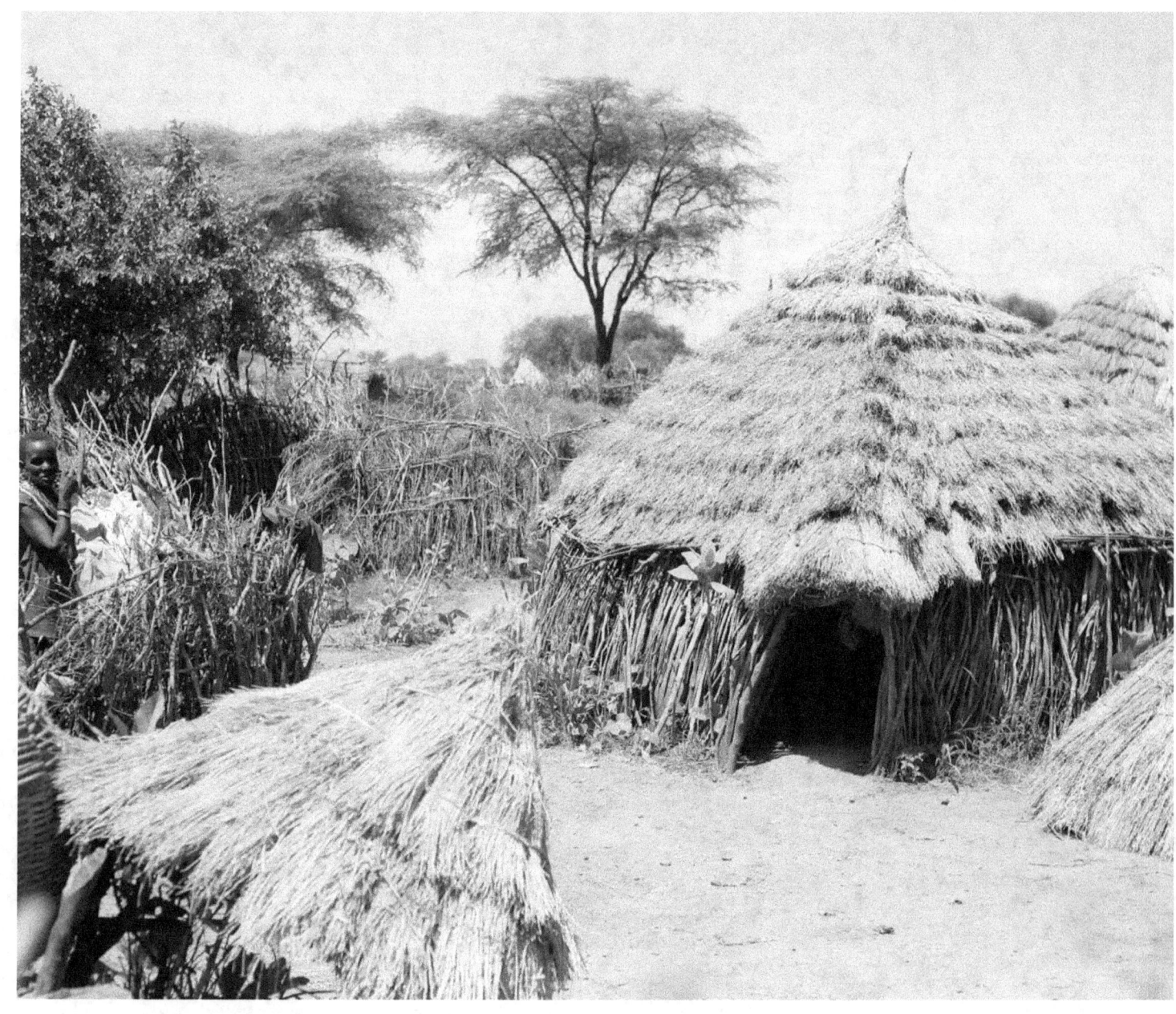

"IT IS FAR BETTER TO BE ALONE, THAN TO BE IN BAD COMPANY."
- GEORGE WASHINGTON

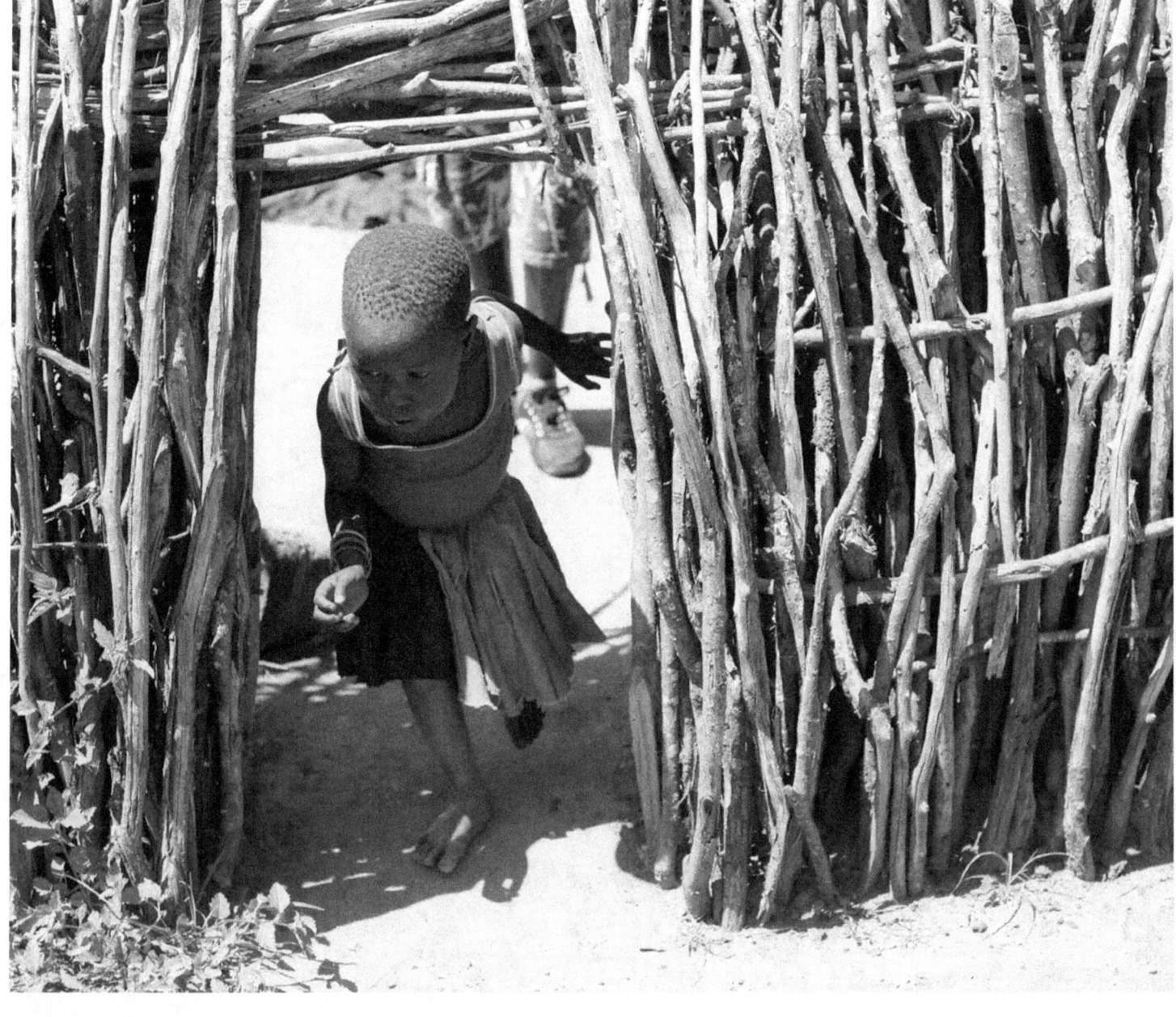

"KEEP YOUR FACE ALWAYS TOWARD THE SUNSHINE – AND SHADOWS WILL FALL BEHIND YOU."
- WALT WHITMAN

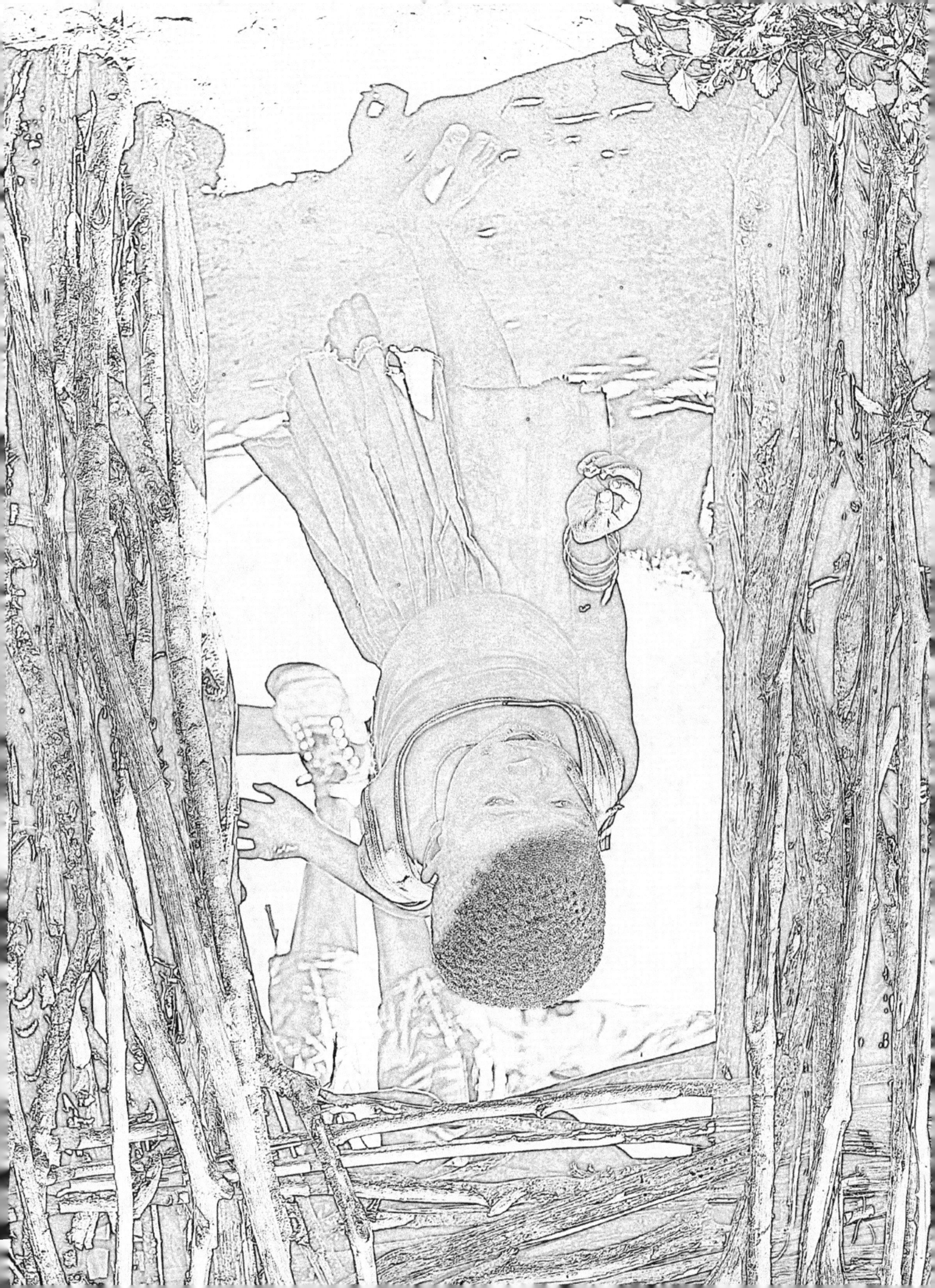

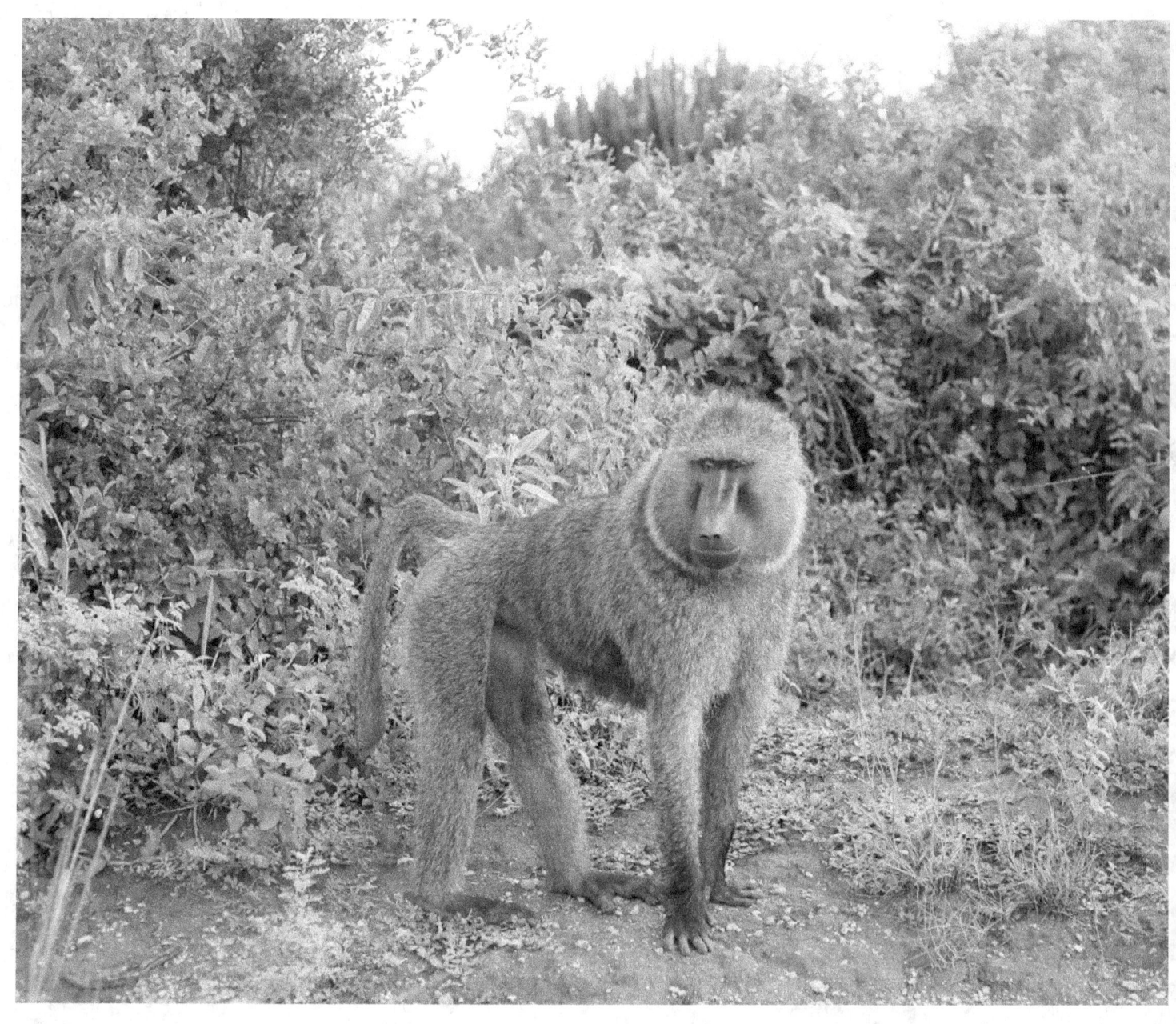

"THE JOURNEY OF A THOUSAND MILES BEGINS WITH ONE STEP."
- LAO TZU

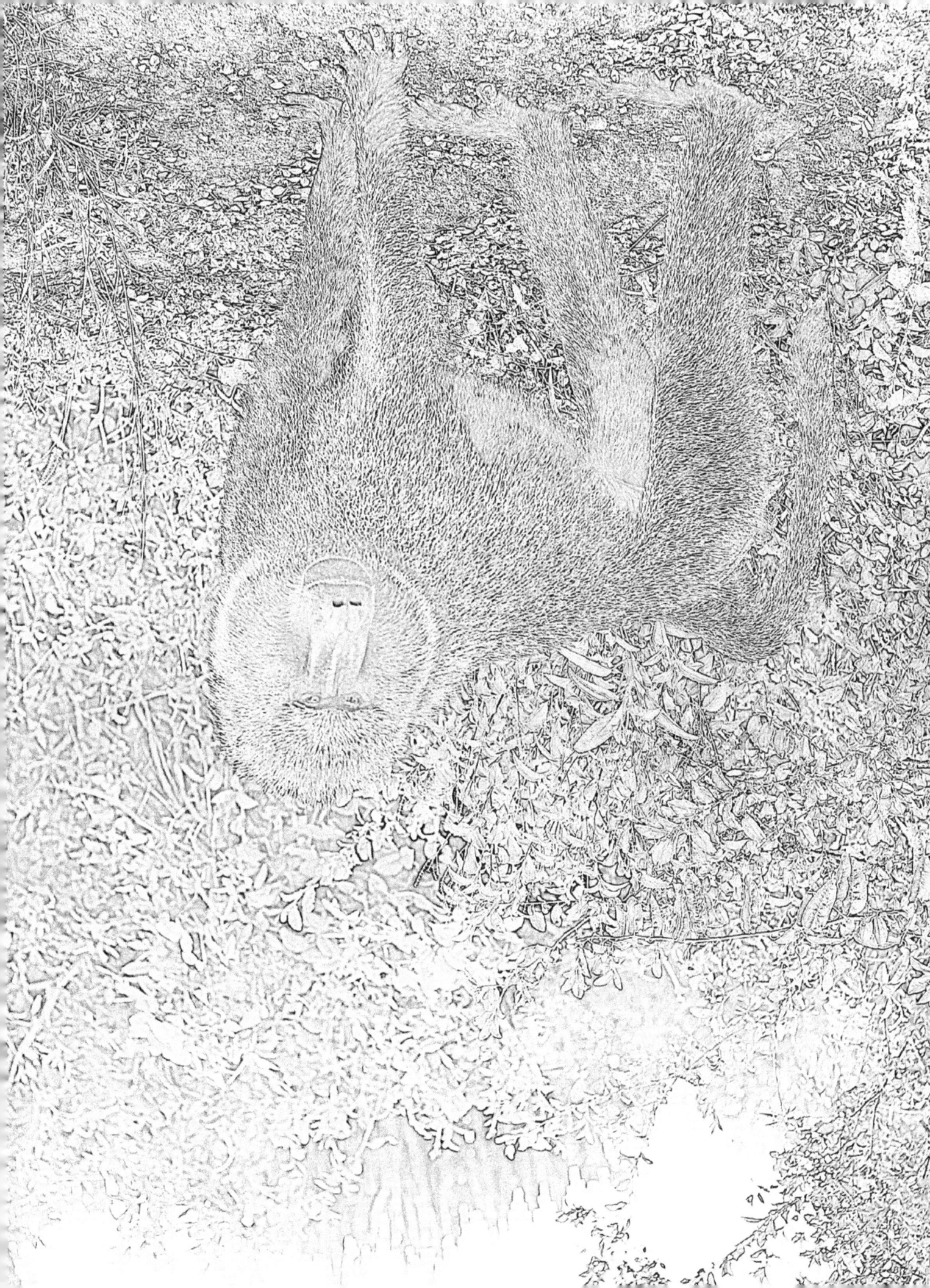

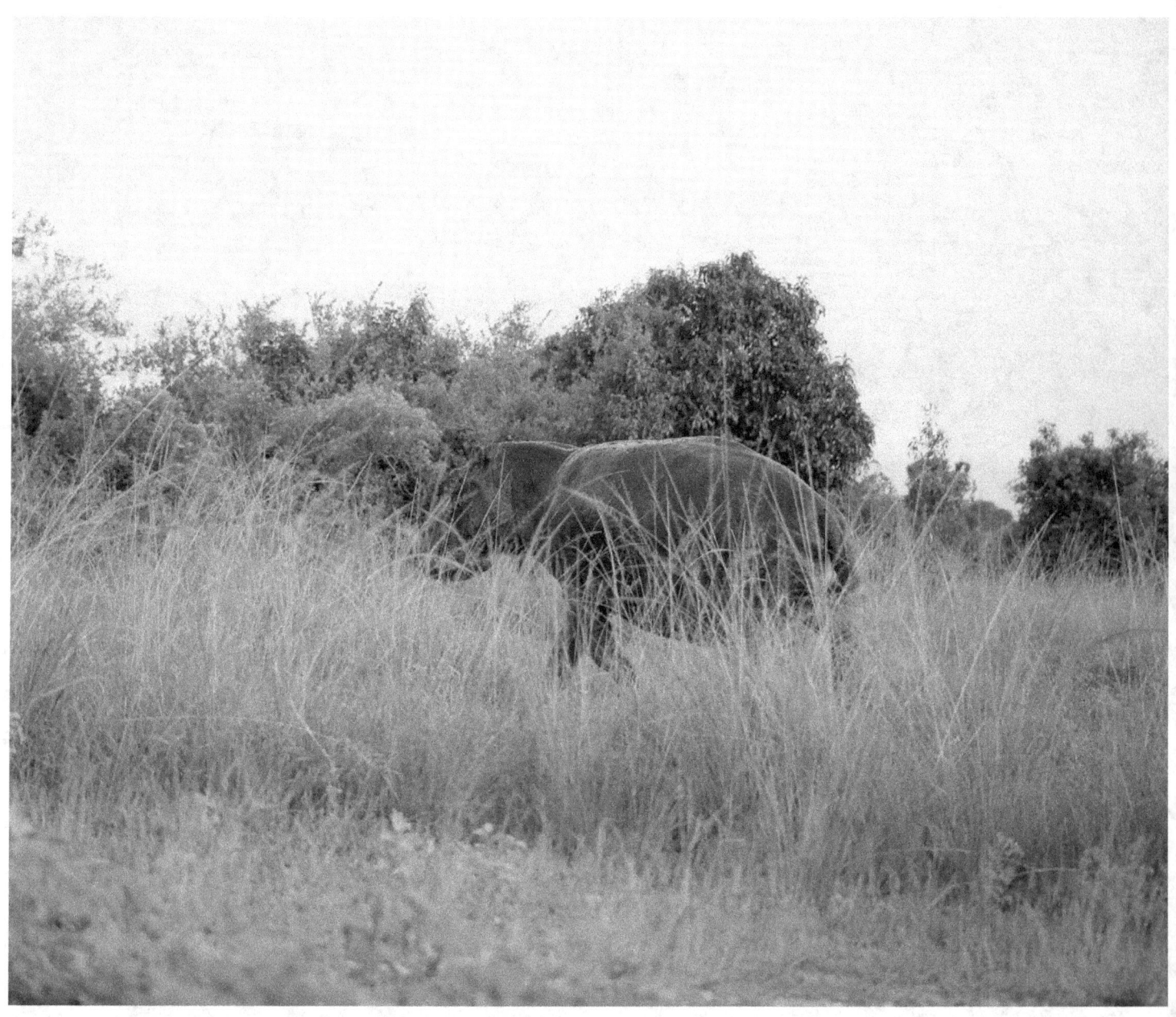

"EVER TRIED. EVER FAILED. NO MATTER. TRY AGAIN. FAIL AGAIN. FAIL BETTER.
- SAMUEL BECKETT

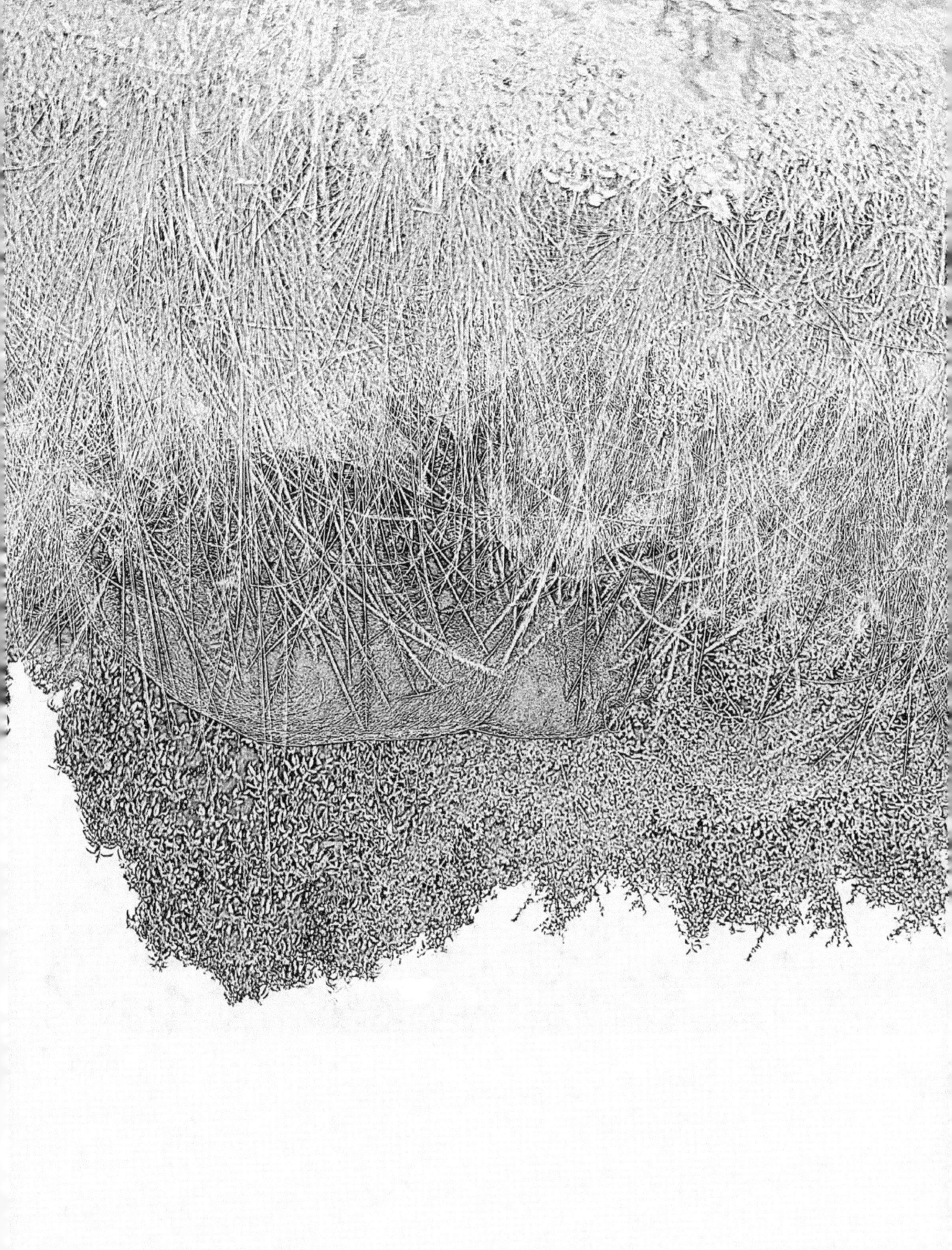

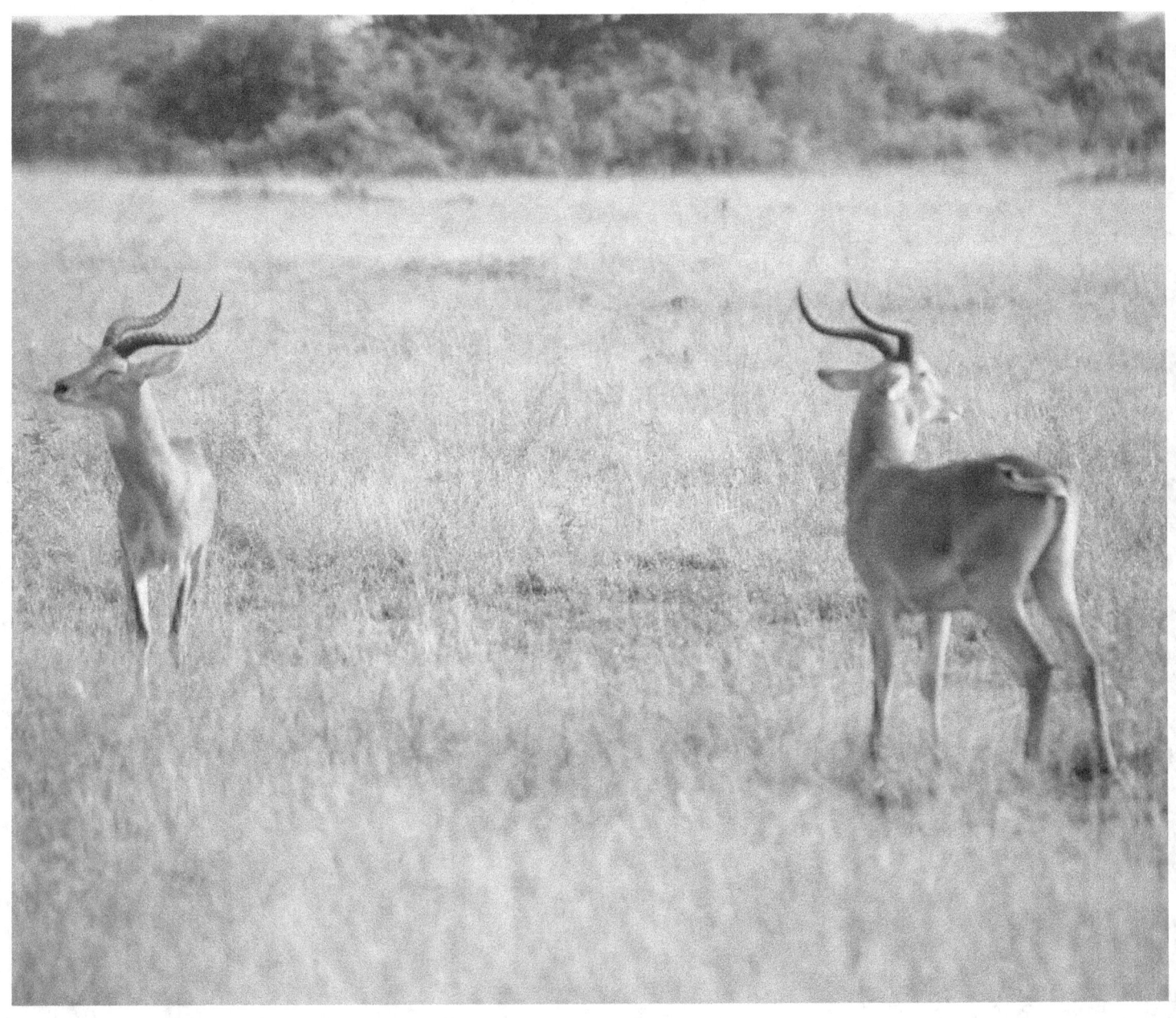

"NOT ALL THOSE WHO WANDER ARE LOST."
- J.R.R. TOLKIEN

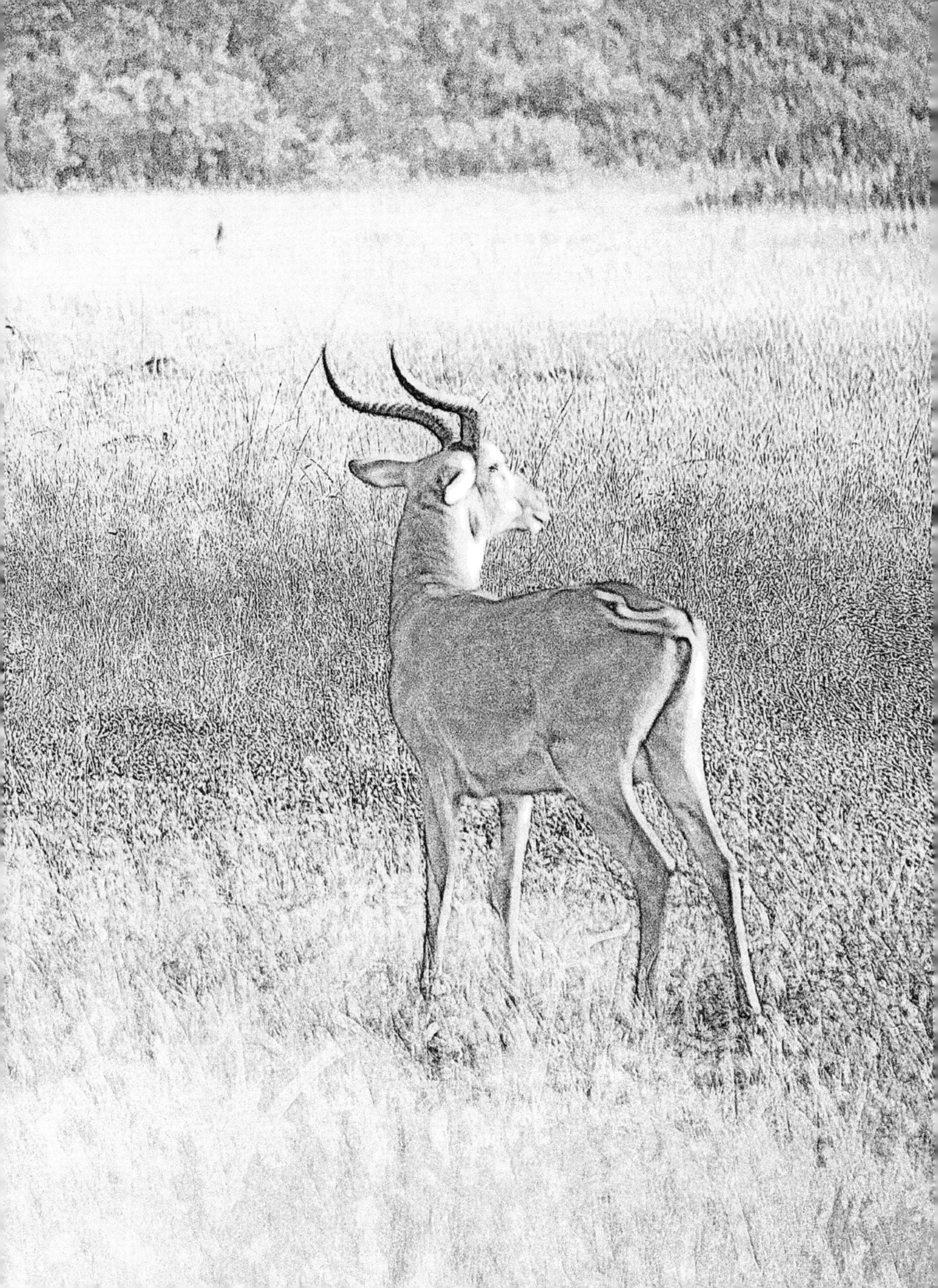

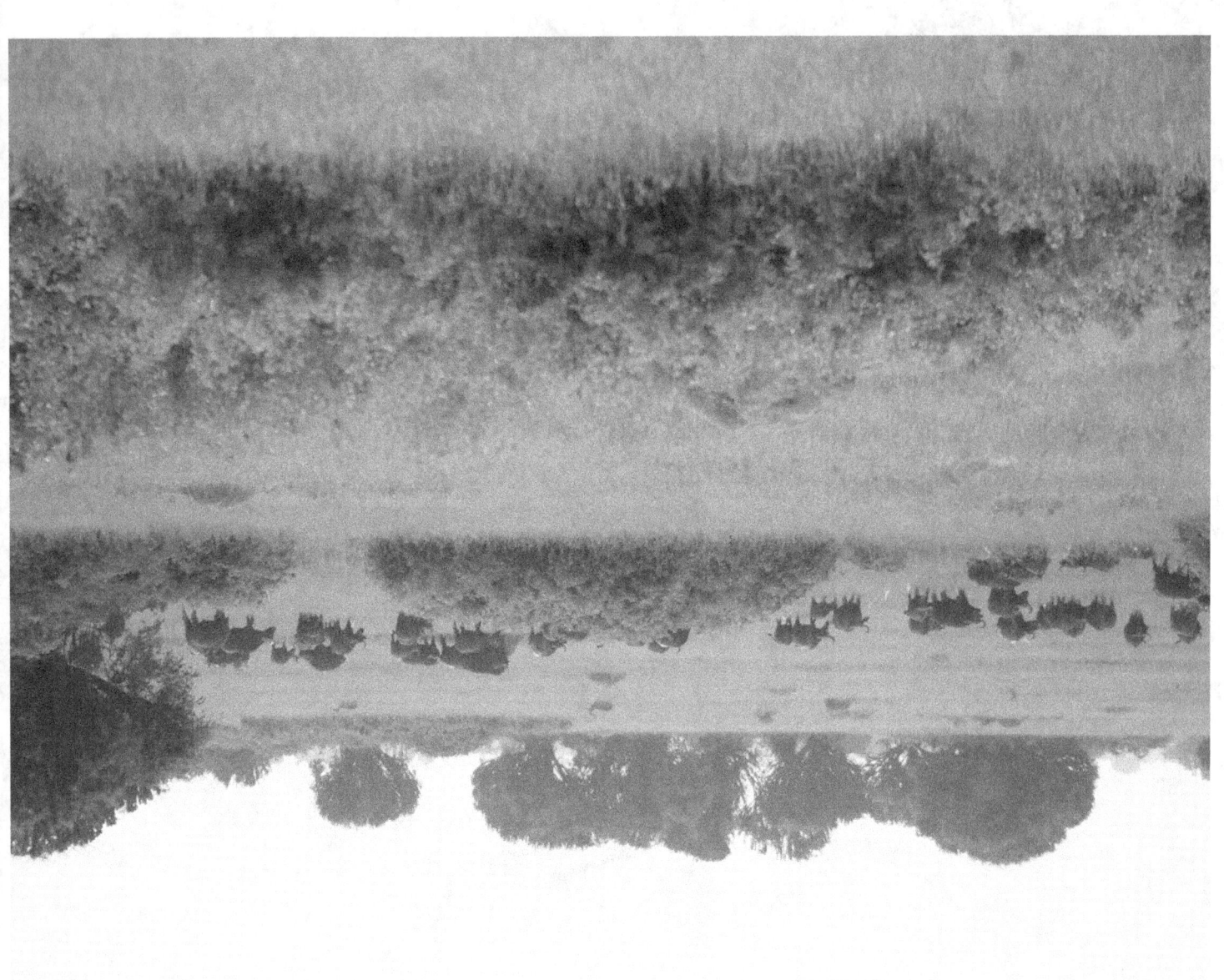

"TELL ME AND I FORGET. TEACH ME AND I REMEMBER. INVOLVE ME AND I LEARN."

- BENJAMIN FRANKLIN

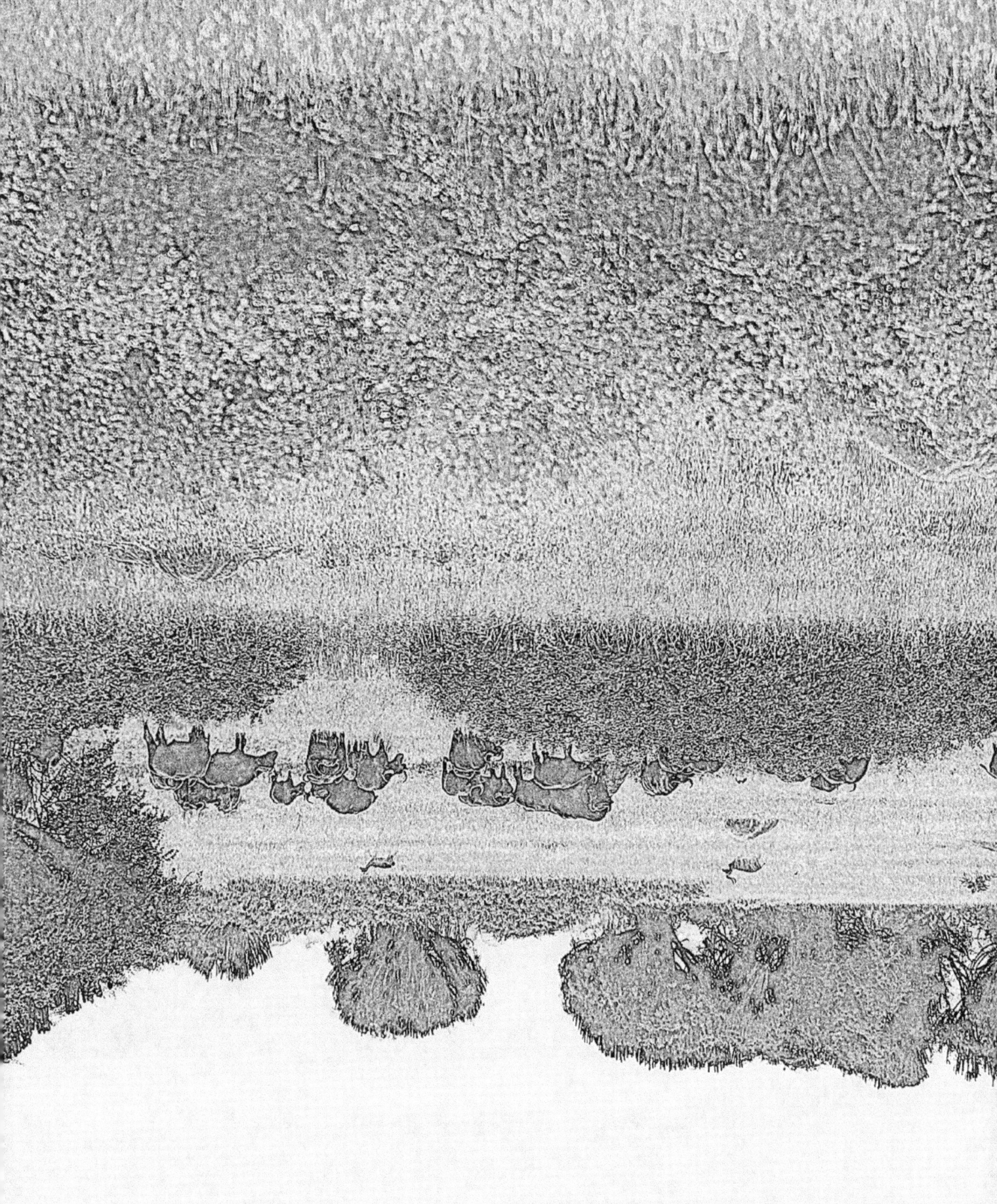

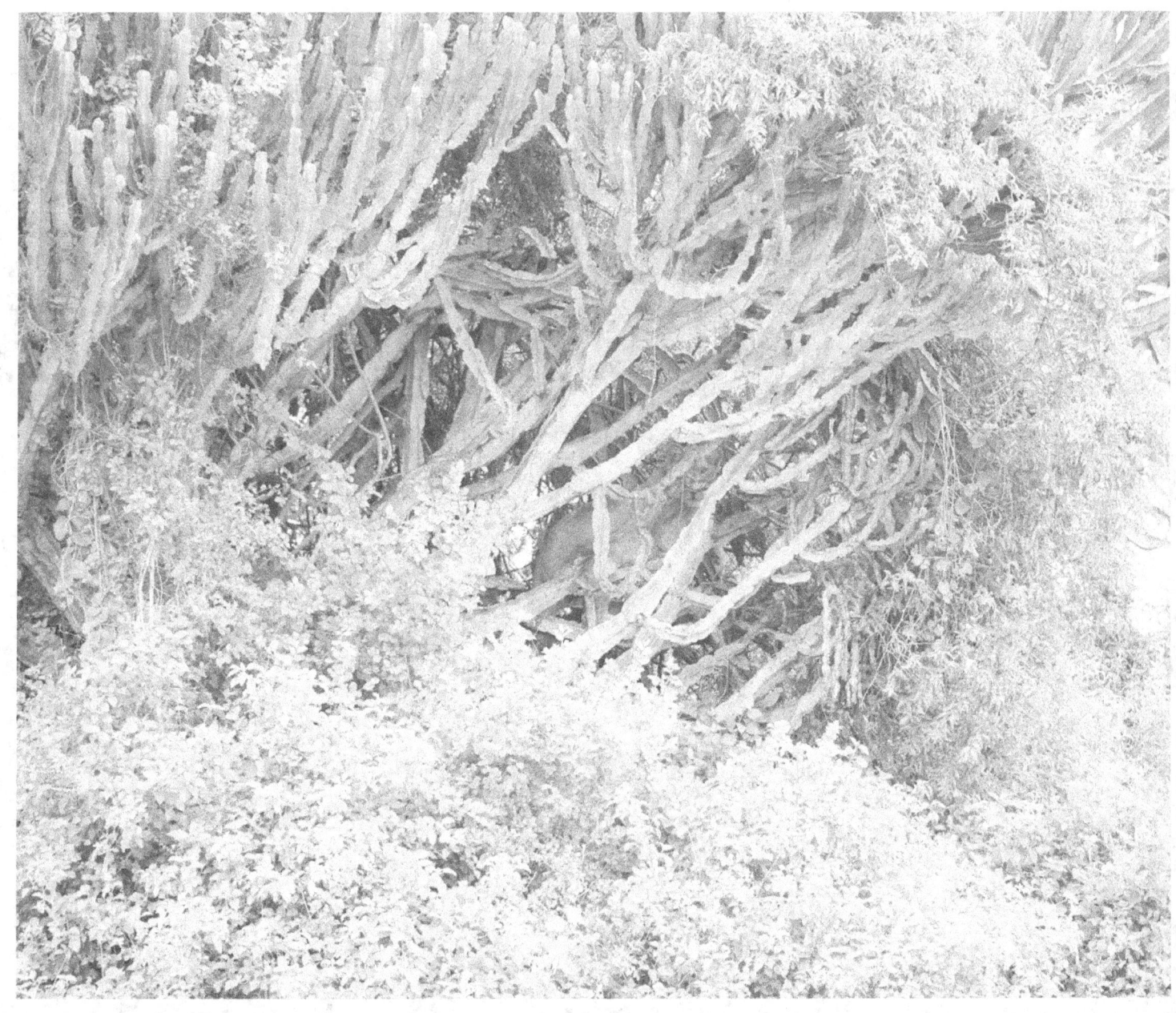

"VERY LITTLE IS NEEDED TO MAKE A HAPPY LIFE; IT IS ALL WITHIN YOURSELF,
IN YOU WAY OF THINKING."
- MARCUS AURELIUS

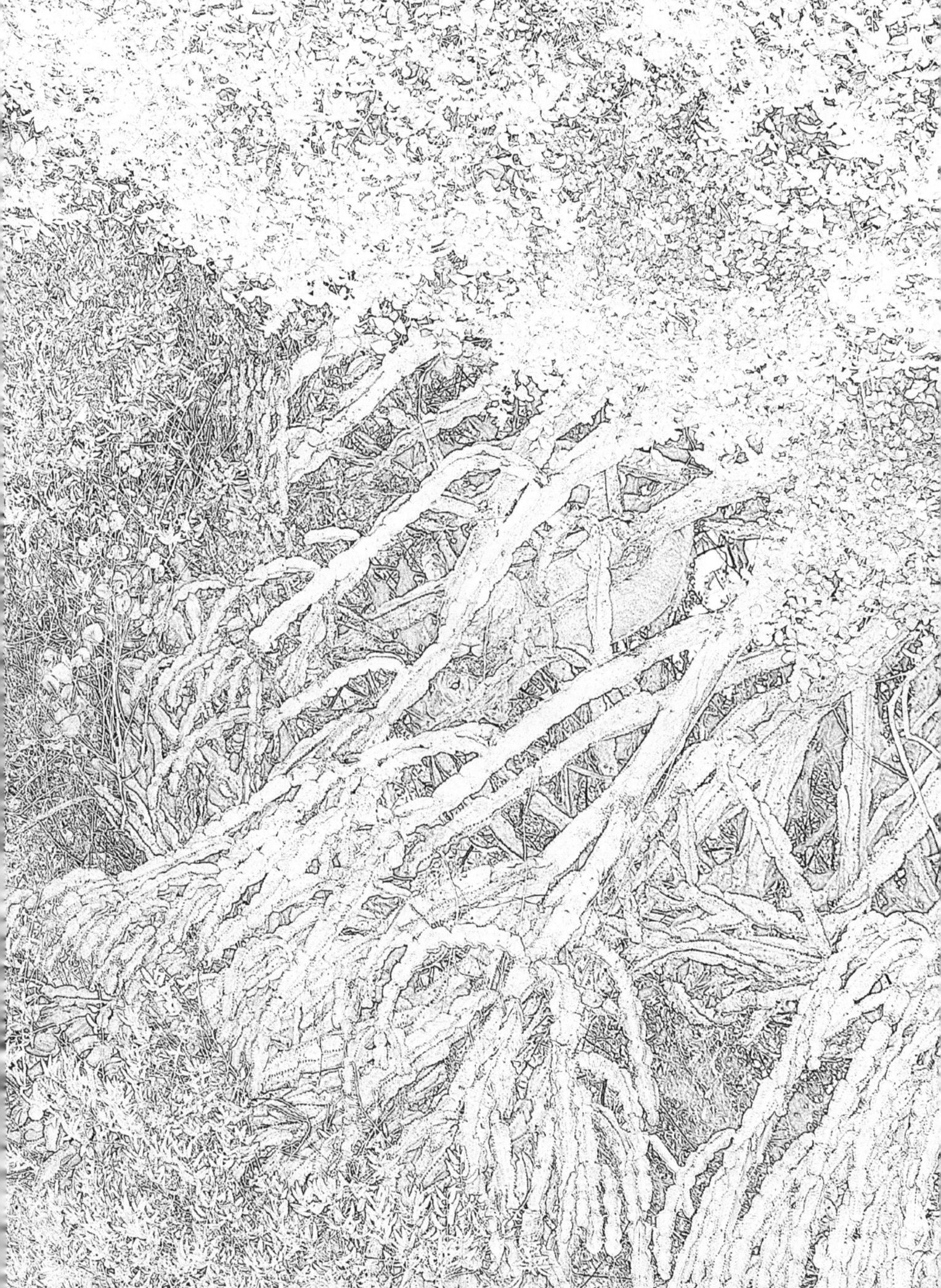

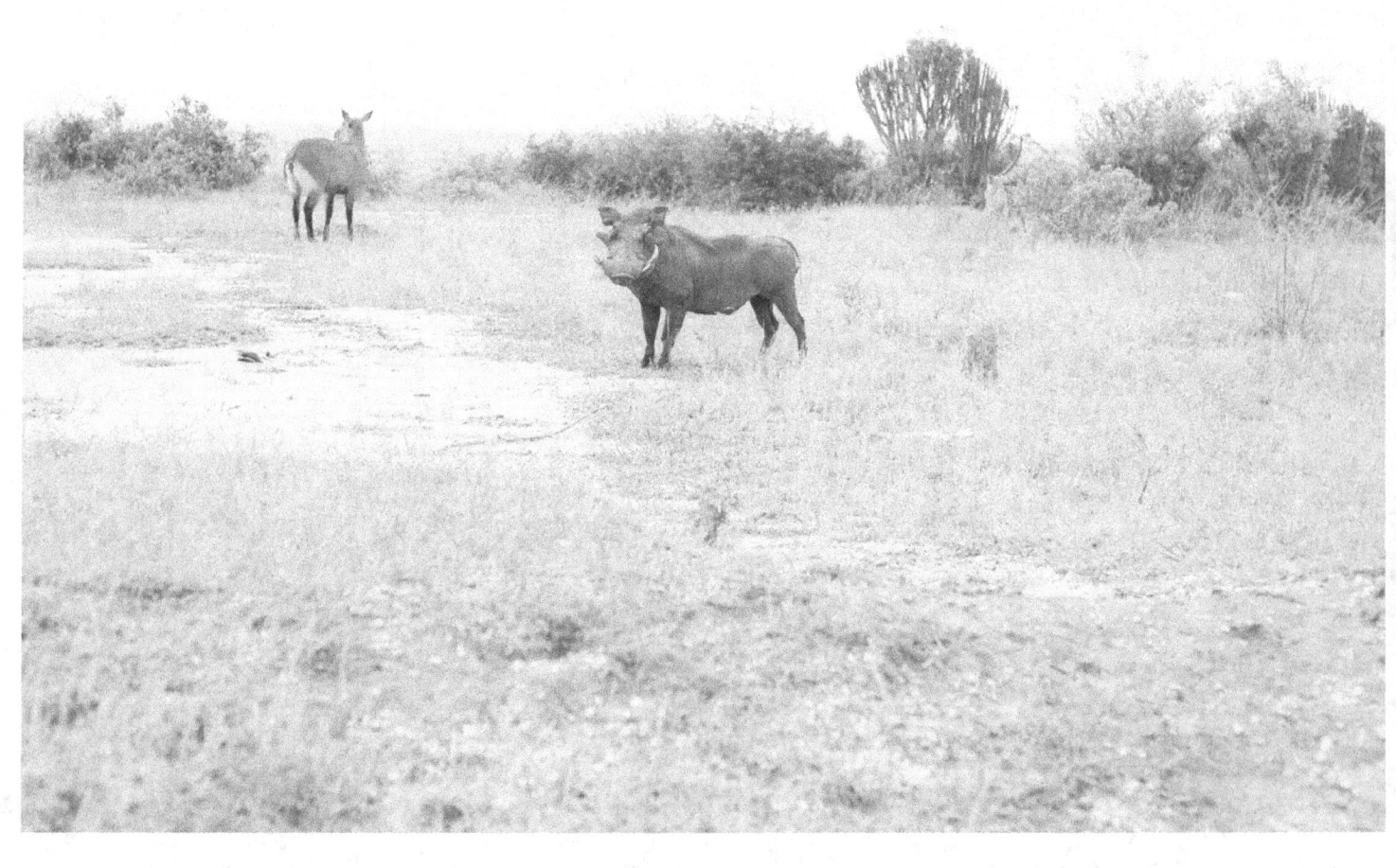

"LET US BE GRATEFUL TO PEOPLE WHO MAKE US HAPPY, THEY ARE THE CHARMING GARDENERS WHO MAKE OUR SOULS BLOSSOM."
- MARCEL PROUST

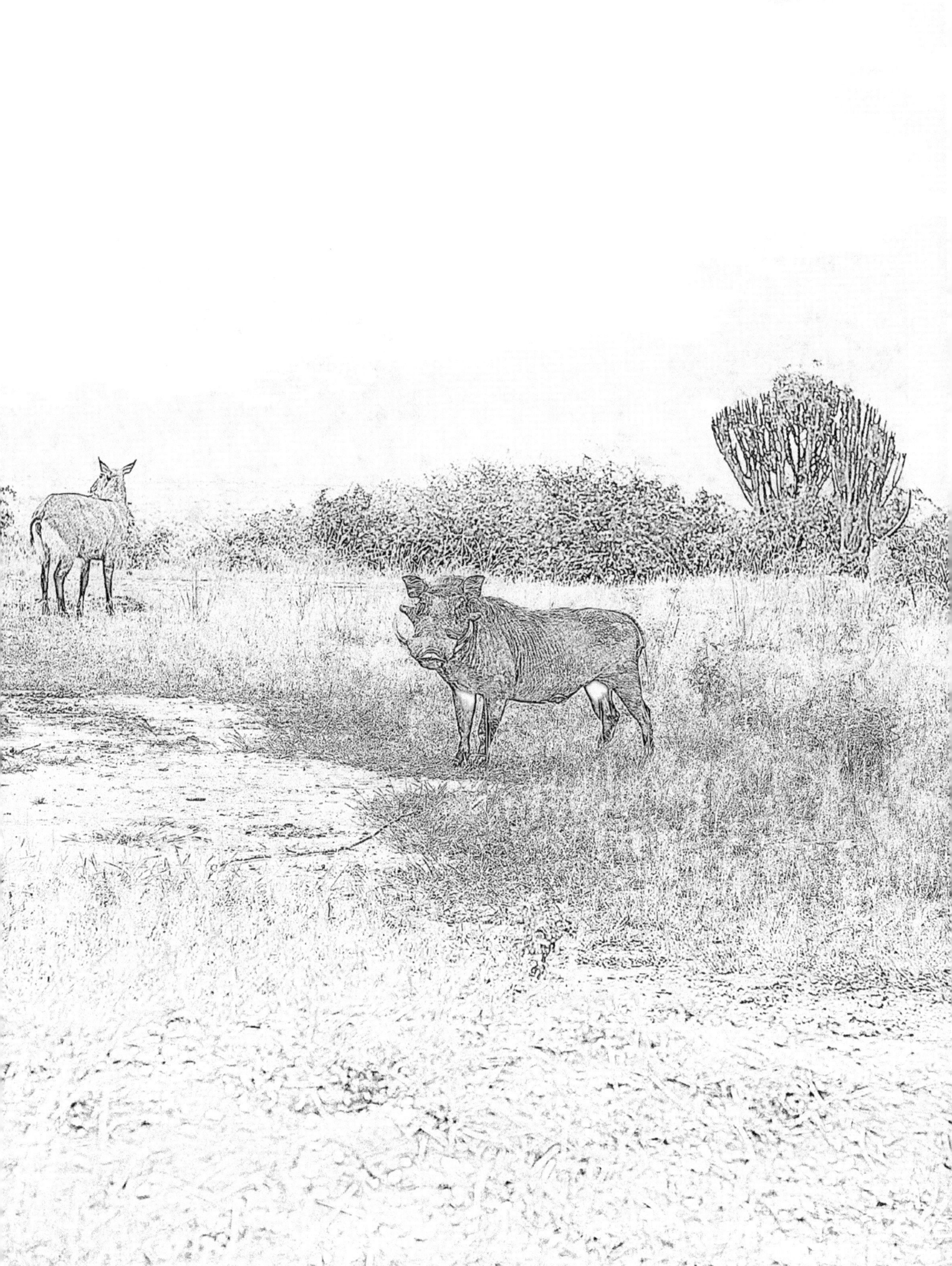

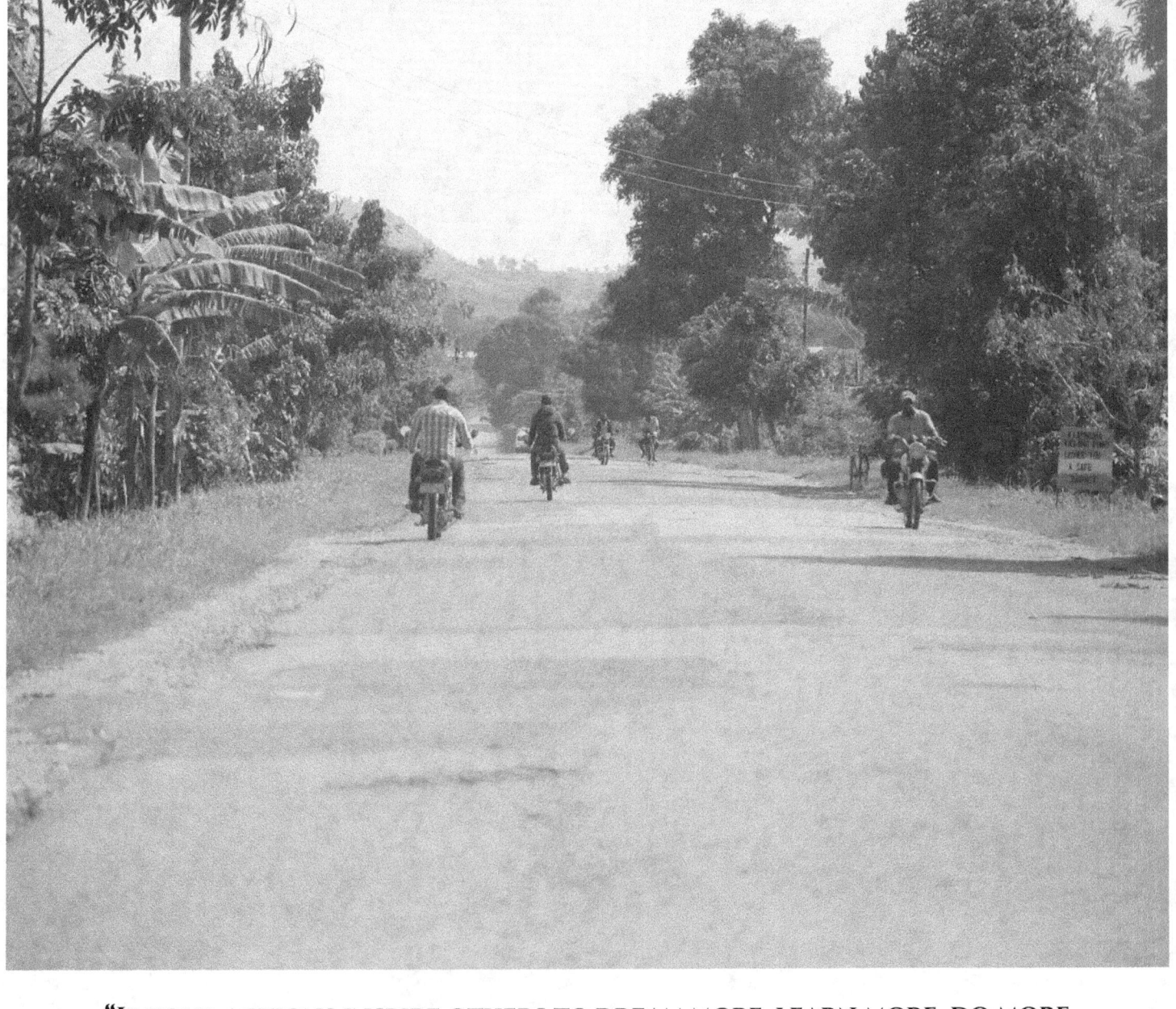

"IF YOUR ACTIONS INSPIRE OTHERS TO DREAM MORE, LEARN MORE, DO MORE
AND BECOME MORE, YOU ARE A LEADER."
- JOHN QUINCY ADAMS

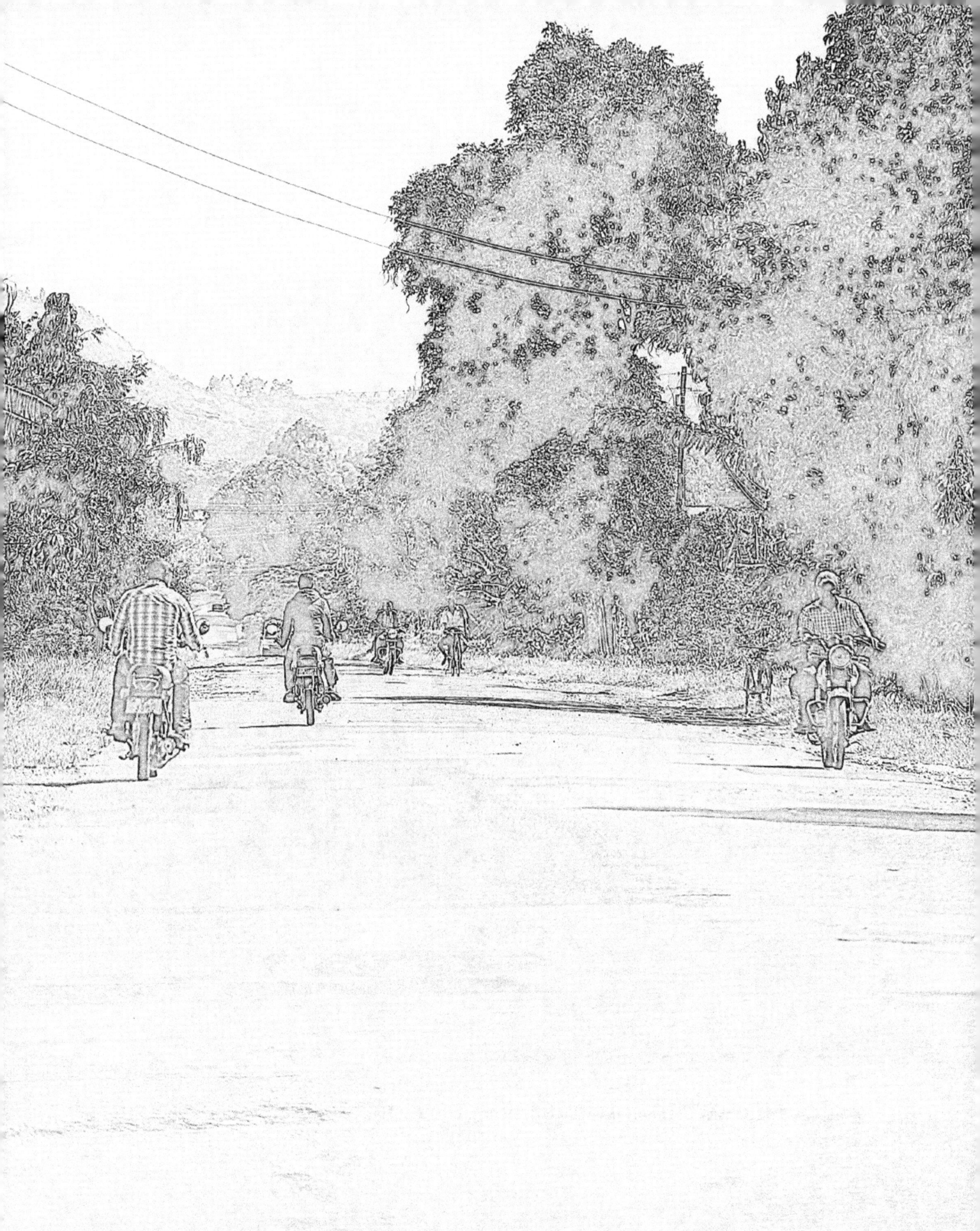

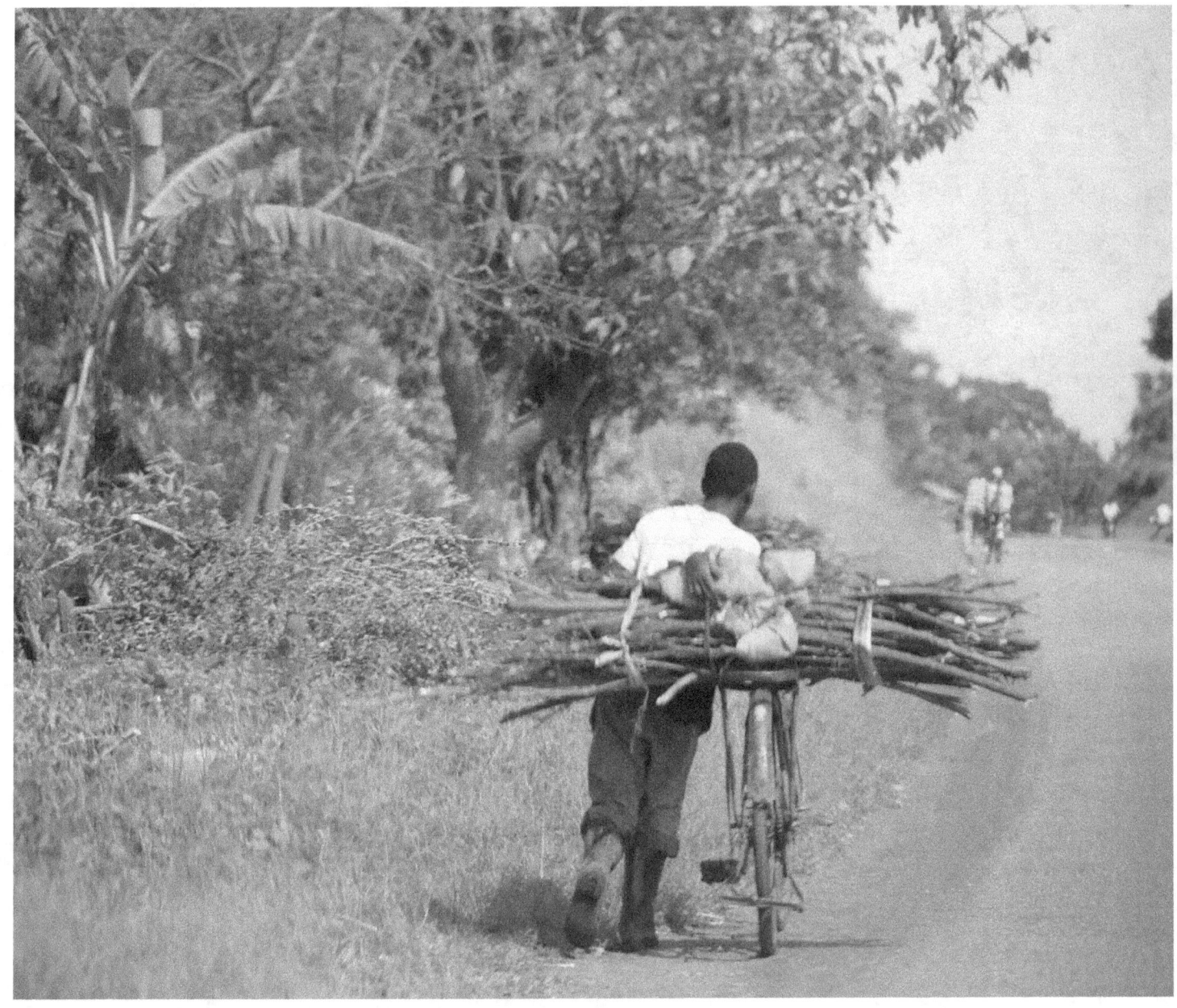

"ALL OUR DREAM CAN COME TRUE, IF WE HAVE THE COURAGE TO PURSUE THEM."
- WALT DISNEY

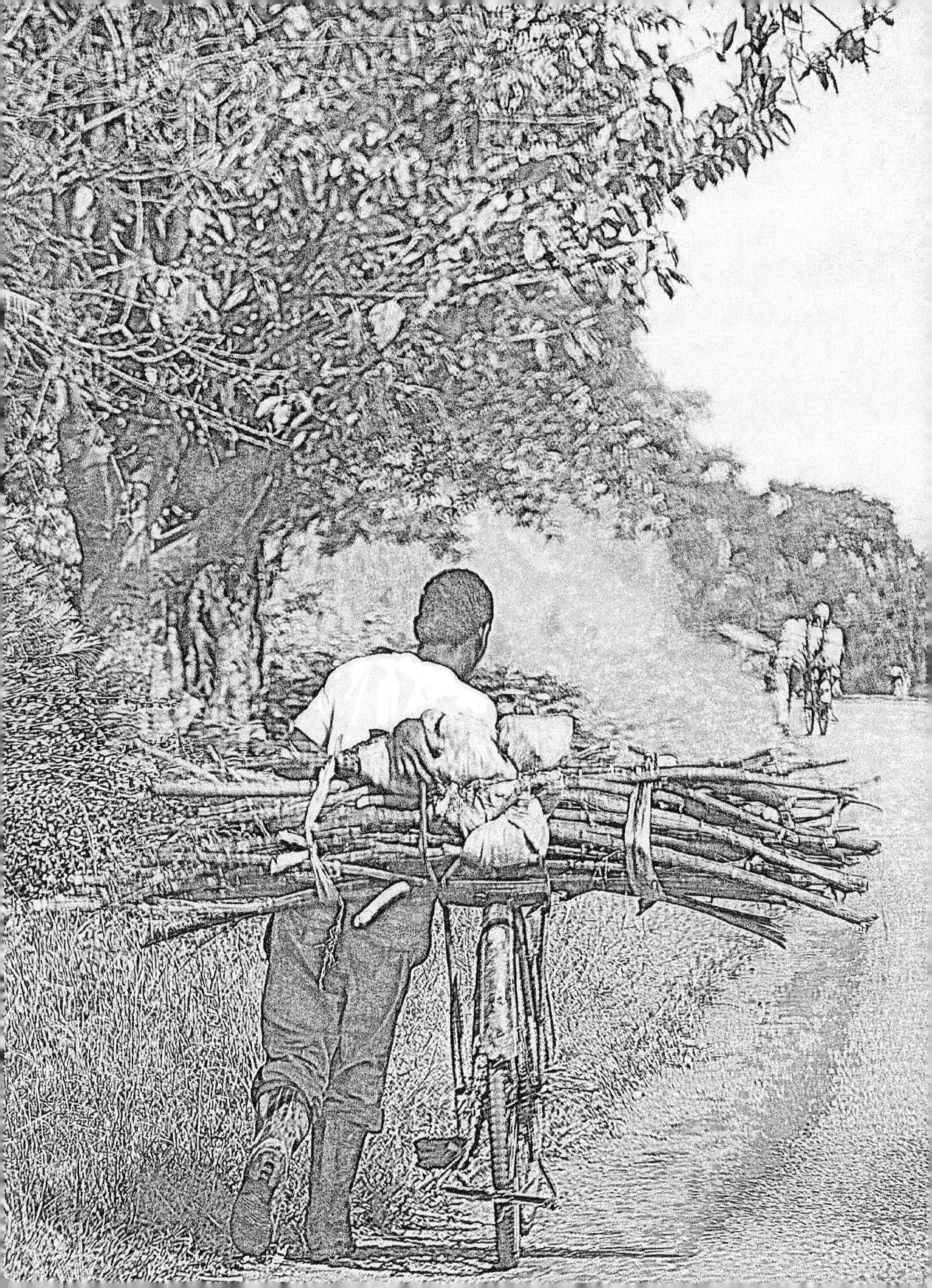

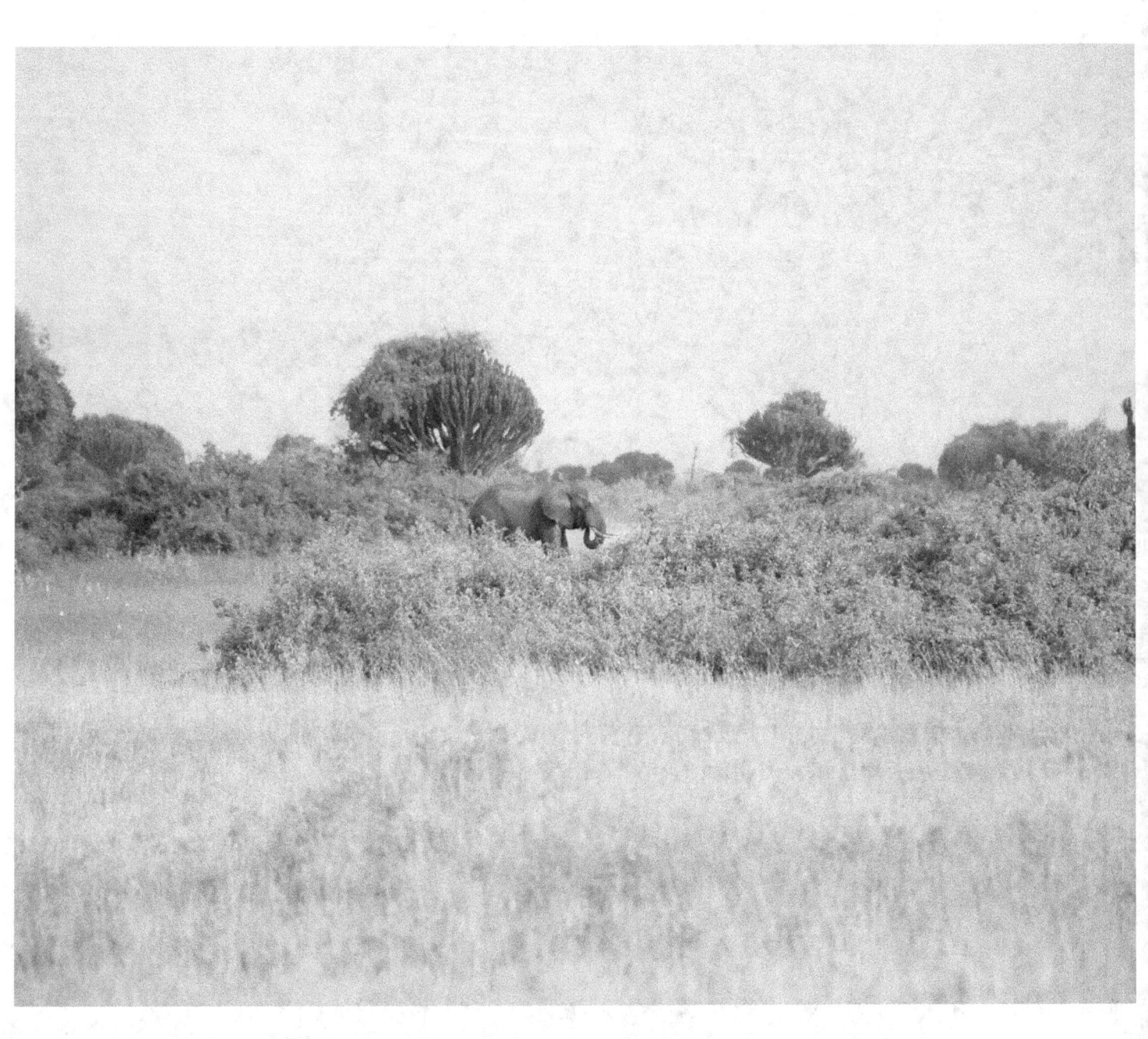

"IT'S NOT WHAT YOU LOOK AT THAT MATTERS, IT'S WHAT YOU SEE."
- HENRY DAVID THOREAU

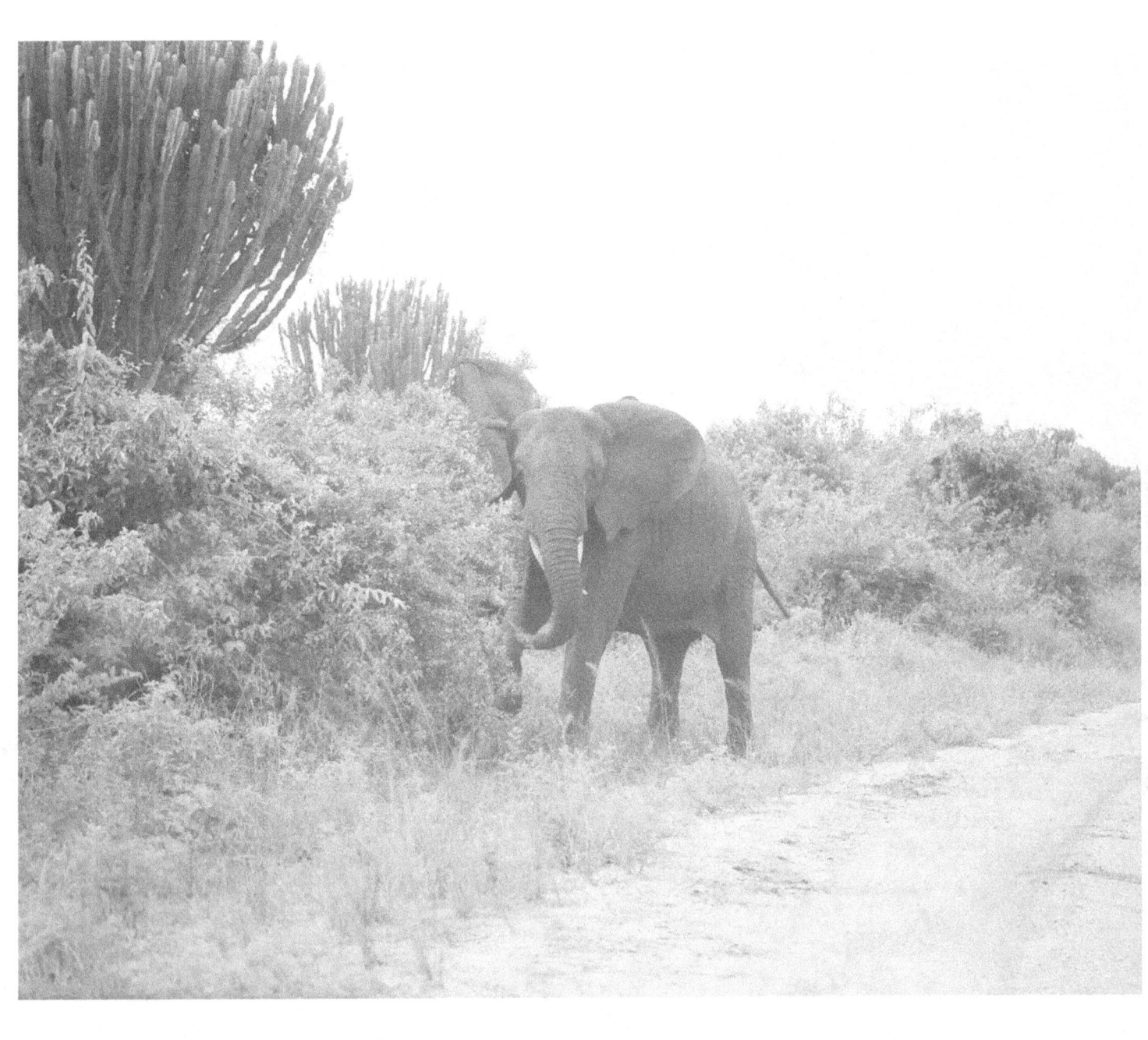

"LIFE IS NOT A PROBLEM TO SOLVED, BUT A REALITY TO BE EXPERIENCE."
- SOREN KIERKEGAARD

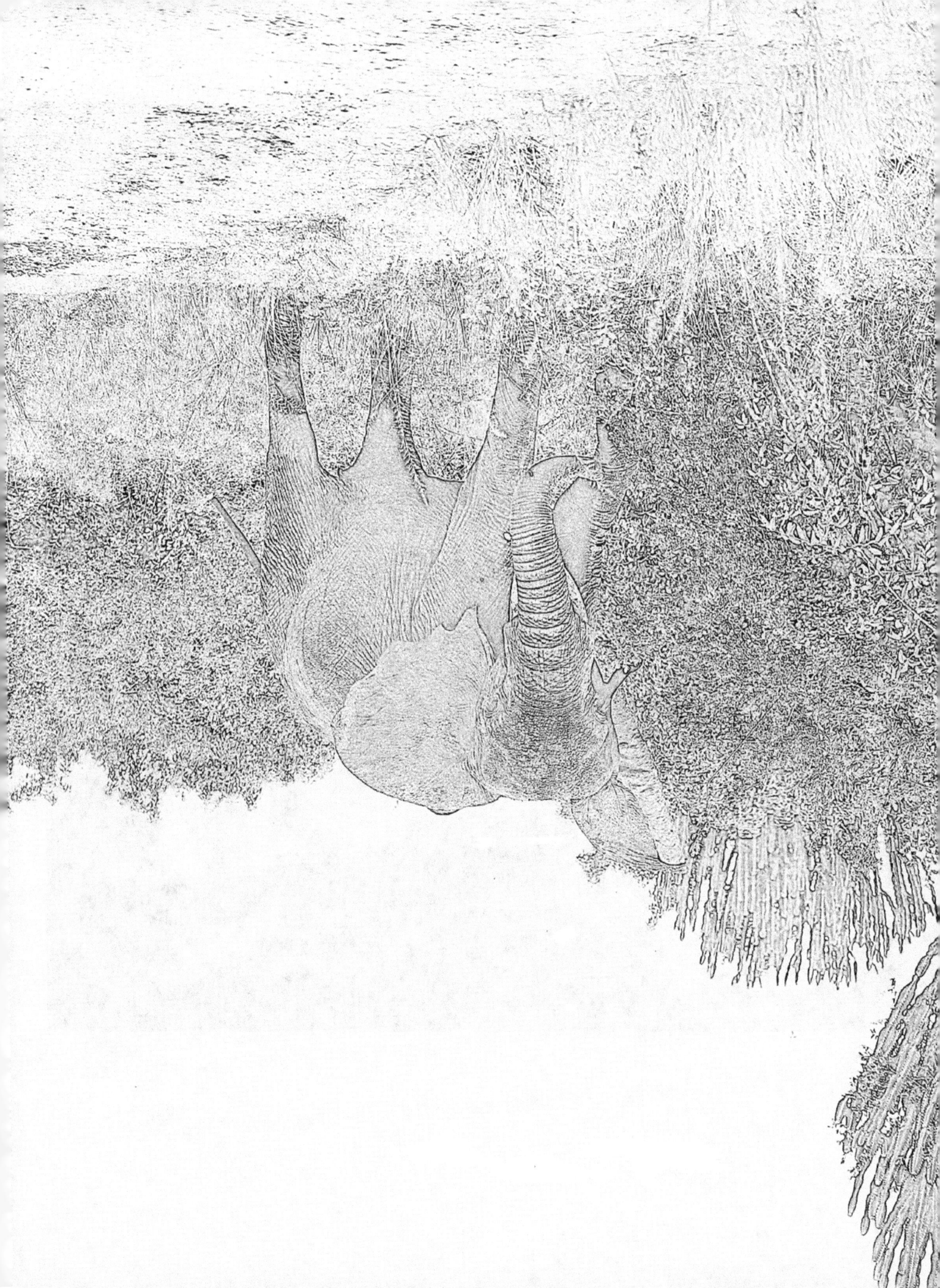

"HAPPINESS RESIDES NOT IN POSSESSIONS, AND NOT IN GOLD,
HAPPINESS DWELLS IN THE SOUL."
- DEMOCRITUS

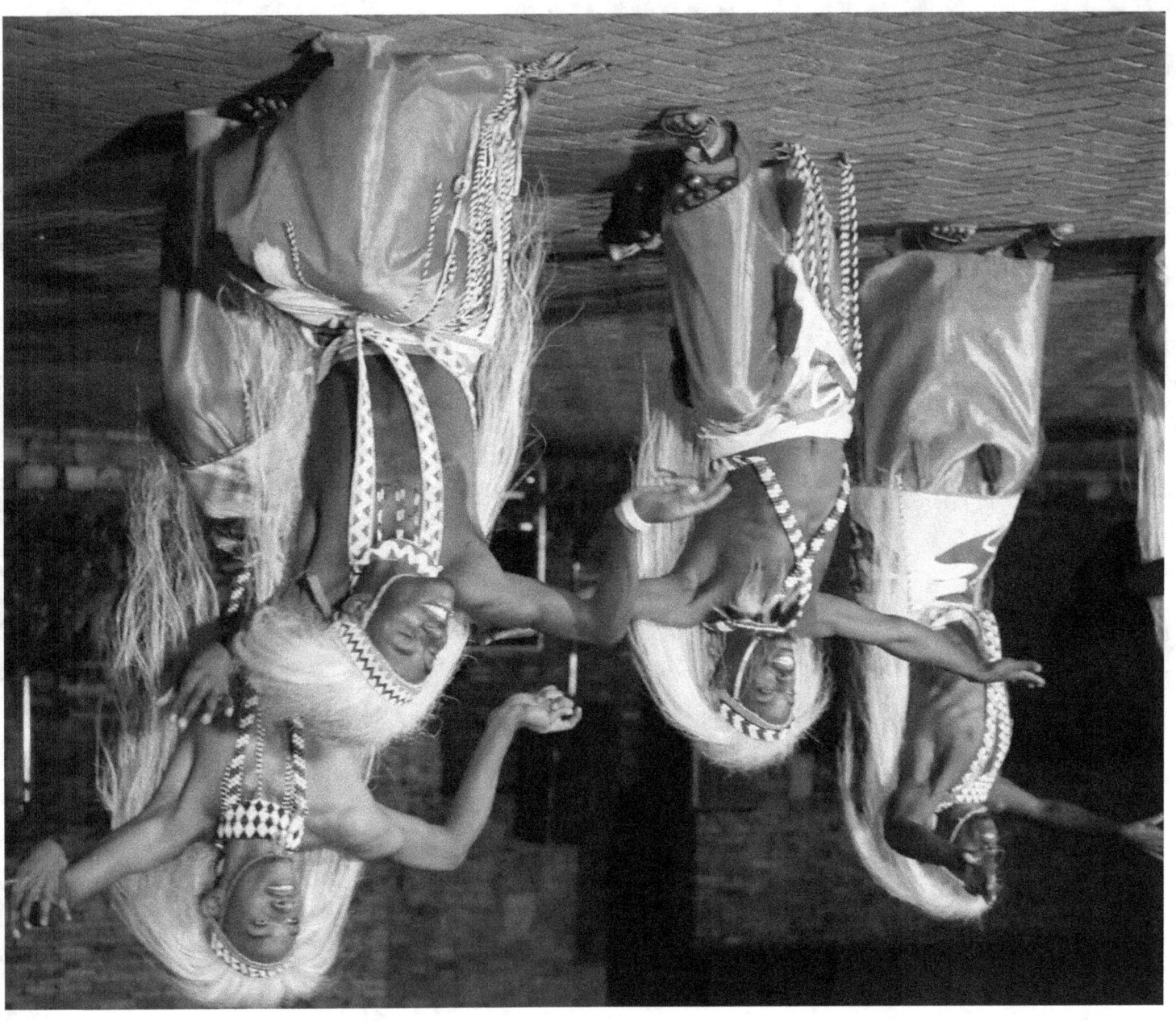

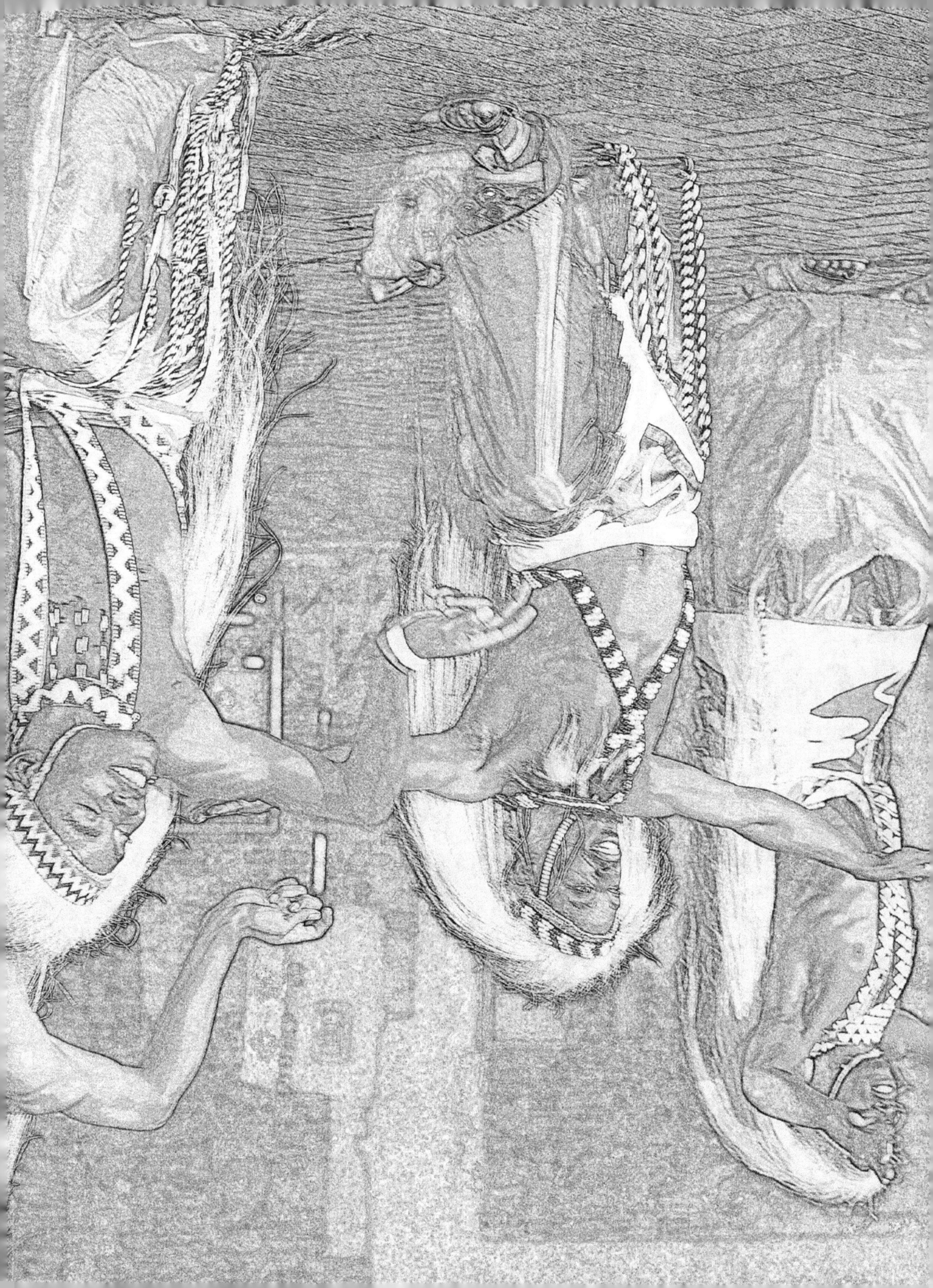

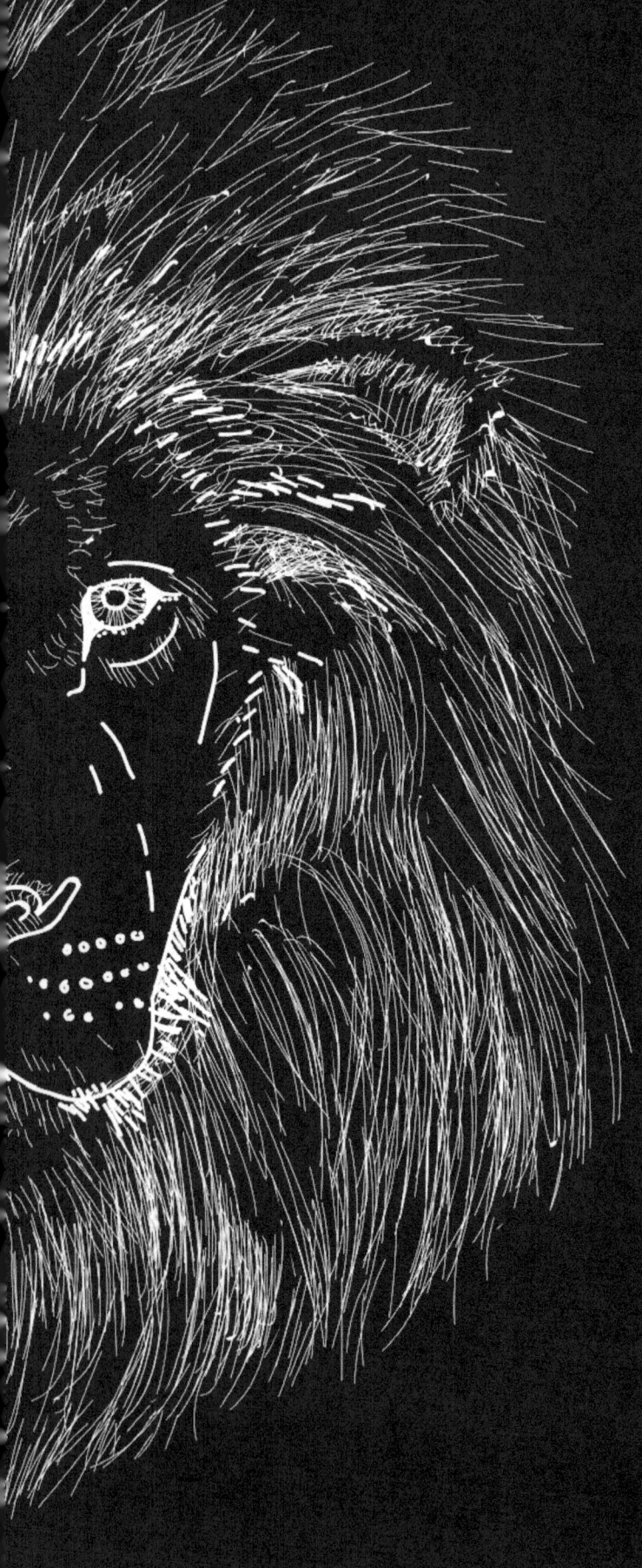

30+ PAGES
TO COLOR FROM AFRICA.

. . . .

CELEBRATE YOUR ARTISTIC ABILITY!

Coloring is an amazing way to relax from the rigors of your day. It helps to take your mind off things that really aren't important. You can color with your child, or a family member to create a new family bond and togetherness that can help to create a connection, zone out during a lunch break, or even something great for you child to work on instead of staring at a TV screen.

The photos enclosed within the coloring book are from the African continent of my personal travels, and photos that I have taken. This being said this isn't just any coloring book, but the scenes, animals and characters are what inspired me to write a book that is to accompany this as well. So on that note coloring becomes more powerful as you're coloring real people, events and animals from a continent that has so much to offer this world.

My dear hope is that you enjoy the photos within and relax with a loved one while connecting with a story through pictures.